"Tim Gombis helps ... stry before he met Jesus, ... d to act on Israel's behalf. ... ll of us engaged in the perilous vocation of shepherding God's flock."

— **Julie Canlis**
author of *Calvin's Ladder*

"Tim Gombis is an outstanding teacher and an expert on Paul. This book confronts the disturbing postures of power that have become prevalent in the church and provides new possibilities for cross-shaped leadership."

— **Brenda DeVries**
pastor at The Journey, Grandville, Michigan

"In *Power in Weakness*, Gombis applies the paradoxical nature of following Jesus (i.e., the way up is down) to Christian leadership. He explores the apostle Paul with pastoral sensitivity and exegetical skill, offering us a Christlike, cross-shaped pattern for leadership."

— **Dennis R. Edwards**
author of *Might from the Margins*

"This is the book I wish I'd read twenty years ago on my way into pastoral ministry. Tim Gombis puts Paul in his own world and helps us see how Paul understood his pastoral ministry."

— **Chris Gonzalez**
president of the Missional Training Center

"*Power in Weakness* blends biblical insight with numerous case studies in real-life ministry today. This is not only one of the best ministry books I have read but an incisive study of Paul's theology as well."

— **Nijay K. Gupta**
author of *Paul and the Language of Faith*

"Gombis not only provides a theology of Paul's ministry but also guides us to think with Paul what it would look like if our churches and leaders truly sought to embody Paul's vision of cruciformity. This is a vision of ministry and pastoral leadership our churches desperately need to hear."

— **Joshua W. Jipp**
author of *Saved by Faith and Hospitality*

"In a time when the charade of political influence, Instagram branding, and hyper-relevance has deformed the church's message, *Power in Weakness* refocuses the task of ministry through a full portrait of Paul as pastor."

— **Darian Lockett**
author of *An Introduction to the Catholic Epistles*

"Rather than offering a philosophy of ministry driven by marketing strategies, borrowing from contemporary leadership techniques, or aiming at mega-churches and celebrity status, this book invites all Christians—and especially pastors—to adopt the cruciformity of Christ in the practices, patterns, and postures of their ministries and life together. May many take heed!"

— **Edward W. Klink III**
senior pastor at Hope Evangelical Free Church, Roscoe, Illinois

"*Power in Weakness* provides a refreshing, transformative, and counter-cultural pathway for pastors to responsibly serve God's people while drawing upon God's resurrection power."

— **Artie M. Lindsay Sr.**
pastor of spiritual formation at Tabernacle Community Church,
Grand Rapids, Michigan

"I had been conditioned to read Paul in a way that excluded his ability to mentor me as pastor. Thankfully, *Power in Weakness* changed that."

— **Carl Ruby**
senior pastor at Central Christian Church, Springfield, Ohio

"For any ministry leader who wrestles with the common temptation of comparison, competition, or control, this book is for you. I recommend it to all Christians, and especially to those whose vocations include equipping the body of Christ for faithful service to the world."

— **AJ Sherrill**
author of *The Enneagram for Spiritual Formation*

"Dr. Gombis rightly focuses his attention on the dynamics of power and weakness in pastoral ministry—Paul's and ours. In my estimation, this is the key to understanding not only Pauline ministry in the first century but pastoral ministry in the twenty-first."

— **Todd Wilson**
president of the Center for Pastor Theologians

"In *Power in Weakness*, Gombis urges the church to be truly claimed by the cross and to be the site of resurrection life through a cruciform posture of self-giving. Some will find it immensely insightful and affirming. Others will find it exceedingly challenging. But everyone needs to read it."

— **Siu Fung Wu**
author of *Suffering in Romans*

"Nothing less than a revolution for our profession."

— **Sharad Yadav**
lead pastor at Bread & Wine, Portland, Oregon

Power in Weakness

Paul's Transformed Vision for Ministry

Timothy G. Gombis

WILLIAM B. EERDMANS PUBLISHING COMPANY
GRAND RAPIDS, MICHIGAN

Wm. B. Eerdmans Publishing Co.
4035 Park East Court SE, Grand Rapids, Michigan 49546
www.eerdmans.com

27 26 25 24 23 22 21   1 2 3 4 5 6 7

ISBN 978-0-8028-7125-1

Library of Congress Cataloging-in-Publication Data

Names: Gombis, Timothy G., 1972– author.
Title: Power in weakness : Paul's transformed vision for ministry /
    Timothy G. Gombis.
Description: Grand Rapids, Michigan : William B. Eerdmans Pub-
    lishing Co., 2021. | Includes bibliographical references and index. |
    Summary: "A guide to pastoral leadership modeled after the Apos-
    tle Paul's ministry"—Provided by publisher.
Identifiers: LCCN 2020026569 | ISBN 9780802871251
Subjects: LCSH: Pastoral theology—Biblical teaching. | Church
    work—Biblical teaching. | Paul, the Apostle, Saint.
Classification: LCC BS2655.P3 G66 2021 | DDC 253—dc23
LC record available at https://lccn.loc.gov/2020026569

For Steve

Contents

A young pastor wrote to me after reading a book I had written on a very similar topic (the apostle Paul's spirituality) that Timothy Gombis unpacks in this book, *Power in Weakness: Paul's Transformed Vision for Ministry*. This pastor said he wanted to embrace a Christlike, Pauline ministerial spirituality, but everyone in his denominational circles was talking about "moving up": going to bigger churches with more staff, larger budgets, and greater influence—until reaching retirement at one of the really big churches in the denomination. This upward mobility was accepted as normal, the standard ministerial path. After all, if the power of God is at work in a church leader (so the argument went), this ascent to greatness is what will naturally happen.

Statistics. Impact. Reputation. Invitations to speak. Influence in the state house or the White House, or at least at city hall. These are the sorts of things by which many people measure the success of pastors and other Christian leaders—and by which those same pastors and other leaders often measure themselves.

This is the kind of minister Paul was, and then was not, argues Tim Gombis. Paul's encounter with the resurrected crucified Jesus transformed him into a pastor who recognized the paradoxical truth that God's resurrection life came—and comes—through the power of the cross. In the strange, counterintuitive ways of God, power is manifest in weakness.

Gombis therefore introduces us to Paul's cross-shaped ministerial spirituality, or cruciformity, and to its critical role in the life of every pastor and every other church leader, as well as each Christian disciple and Christian community. As both a scholar and a pastoral leader, Gombis plumbs the depths of Paul's practical theology and perceptively analyzes the state of ministry in much of the church in the West. His understanding of Paul is profound, his analysis of ministry more than a bit concerning. Something must change. The church needs a conversion of its "ministry imagination." Readers will find that Paul, in the hands of our author, can guide us into that conversion.

My wife and I have never been part of a perfect church or had a perfect pastor. We have, however, been blessed to have had pastors, both men and women, whose ministries were life-giving because they were cross-shaped. That is, they embodied the truth the following pages explore in depth: that Christ's resurrection life comes through lives of cruciformity.

The Pauline pastor, Gombis compellingly demonstrates, is the cruciform pastor, and vice versa. The apostle Paul attempted to embody a life-giving, cross-shaped ministry and to urge others, by example and word, to embody that same type of ministry. It was his *modus operandi*. The words of Paul and the words of Tim work together in this book to offer us a fresh, compelling vision of ministry for the contemporary church. Let those who have ears to hear, hear.

Michael J. Gorman
St. Mary's Seminary & University

This book is an extended meditation on the dynamics of power and weakness in pastoral ministry. While many things can and should be said about ministers and service to the church, I have attempted to offer a targeted and strategic contribution by examining contemporary ministry in light of the dramatic reversal of Paul's life when the exalted Lord Jesus confronted him on the Damascus Road. That encounter shattered and recreated everything about Paul, transforming his theology, reconfiguring his life and radically reshaping his mode of ministry. He turned from a quest for power and prestige toward a new pursuit of conformity to the cross of Christ. This cruciform approach affected his self-understanding, his consideration of his mission partners and his posture toward the churches to which he sent letters.

This specific focus on power and weakness in ministry distinguishes my contribution from several other excellent works on Paul as a pastor, two of which appeared while I was completing this manuscript. Scot McKnight's recent and lively work, *Pastor Paul*, takes a broader view of Paul's approach to ministry through the lens of *Christoformity*, a notion closely related to *cruciformity*.[1] His sketch of Paul's aims in ministry to cultivate in the church a culture of conformity to Christ resonates strongly with my work. James Thompson likewise considers the transformational dynamics in Paul's pastoral approach in his insightful *Pastoral Ministry according to Paul*.[2] These

1. Scot McKnight, *Pastor Paul: Nurturing a Culture of Christoformity in the Church* (Grand Rapids: Brazos Press, 2019).
2. James W. Thompson, *Pastoral Ministry according to Paul: A Biblical Vision* (Grand Rapids: Baker Academic, 2006).

two resources from world-class New Testament scholars, both of whom are intensely interested in the life of the church, are profound gifts. Another volume that richly repays careful reading is the collection of essays on a variety of topics in *Paul as Pastor*, edited by Brian Rosner, Andrew Malone and Trevor Burke.[3] I would be delighted if my contribution to pastors—a reflection on the manner in which a cruciform vision renovated Paul's life and ministry—took a place alongside these other significant volumes.

Reflecting on Paul's theology of cruciformity—life and ministry in the shape of the cross—has profoundly transformed every aspect of my life. It has been a serious delight to see the cross claim more and more of my life, for this has led to my increased enjoyment of resurrection power. This has brought about life-giving changes in my family life and friendships in more wonderful ways than I can possibly recount. It has also guided my teaching of ministers and those headed for service to the church. This book is an attempt to capture and articulate that vision of the life-giving power of the cross as it pertains to pastoral ministry.

I learn through conversation and partnerships. So many friends have helped to shape the ideas in the following pages. My doctoral supervisor at the University of St. Andrews, Bruce Longenecker, first introduced me to the manner in which Paul's thought and life are shaped by the cross. And I have learned much through the writing of Michael Gorman, especially his *Cruciformity* and *Inhabiting the Cruciform God*.[4] I am delighted and deeply honored that he agreed to contribute a foreword to this book.

I am grateful for my good friend Michael Thompson, who acquired this book for Eerdmans. Though he has now moved on to

---

3. Brian S. Rosner, Andrew S. Malone and Trevor J. Burke, eds., *Paul as Pastor* (London: T&T Clark, 2017).

4. Michael J. Gorman, *Cruciformity: Paul's Narrative Spirituality of the Cross* (Grand Rapids: Eerdmans, 2001); *Inhabiting the Cruciform God: Kenosis, Justification, and Theosis in Paul's Narrative Soteriology* (Grand Rapids: Eerdmans, 2009).

another publisher, I deeply appreciate his patience and encouragement, especially at a crucial juncture when I felt the project was falling apart. My thanks are due to James Ernest at Eerdmans for guiding it through the final stages.

Many friends read previous drafts and offered generous and constructive criticism, saving me from errors large and small. Elizabeth Davidhizar engaged me in vigorous dialogue about many things, but especially the contours and challenges of cruciformity. Jennifer Reil offered extensive editorial help and many helpful suggestions, as did Natalie Kompik. Pastor Brenda DeVries has been a faithful conversation partner for some time now in the study of the New Testament and the challenges of serving the church. I am deeply grateful for these women in ministry from whom I have learned much and who have been my partners in learning from Paul. Pastor Lance Walker proved to be a faithful friend with routine and persistent encouragement. Pastor Andrew Bolkcom likewise offered generous comments and constructive criticism, as did pastors Andrew Kischner, Jackie Whyte, and Steve Van Poolen.

I am grateful to my life partner, Sarah, for helping me sketch the plan of the book and encouraging me throughout the project. My mother, Kathryn Gombis, and my sisters, Alison Hall and Leah Bare also read drafts and provided editorial help. I am happy to share with all of these partners any good accomplished by this book while I alone am responsible for its shortcomings.

I worked on portions of this book during a sabbatical stay at Ridley Hall, Cambridge, a restful season I recall with great fondness. Many thanks are due to Kurt Behrends of the Issachar Fund, who offered generous support for my travels. My dean at Grand Rapids Theological Seminary, John VerBerkmoes, a peerless servant-leader, made possible a semester leave and also provided significant funding. His leadership enables me to enjoy a comfortable life of scholarship and teaching and I deeply appreciate his friendship.

Words cannot capture what my friend, Steve Watkins, means to me. My life would be quite different, and much impoverished, without him. Our conceptions of life and ministry have developed along similar lines over the last two and a half decades and much of my vision of many things is due to our ongoing rich conversations. His imprint marks not only my life but nearly every page of this book. I dedicate it to him with great love and affection.

Paul's encounter with the risen Christ on the road to Damascus radically transformed his pastoral ministry. In an instant his world was shattered, along with his certainties about himself and his understanding of the God of Israel. He discovered that his approach to shepherding God's people to love and obey God's word for God's glory had somehow set him *against* God. Something had to give. Everything, as it turned out, needed to change. In light of Paul's encounter with the exalted Lord Jesus Christ on that midday near Damascus, Paul's mode of ministry was dramatically altered—his approach to people, his evaluation of others, his regard for ministry partners, his self-identity, his concern for social status and so much more.

The conversion of Paul on the Damascus road is a famous biblical episode. Represented in art and literature, it forms the basis for so many personal faith narratives. But this moment and Paul's subsequent life and ministry have not often been seen as a rich resource for considering what we can learn about pastoral ministry. In this book I will reflect on just what changed in that moment and how that transformation can shape how we conceive of faithfully shepherding God's people today.

A Personal and Pastoral Transformation

About a decade ago, a season of intense ministry created a perfect storm of trouble that left me utterly exhausted. I chaired the leadership team in our church and was growing impatient, increasingly frustrated and, to be honest, angry at some fellow leaders who were raising serious questions about the direction of our church and the nature of our shared vision. This came at the same time as a season of

1

institutional unrest at the college where I was then teaching. Adding
to my stress were looming deadlines on some writing projects that
I could hardly find the time to work on because I was giving so much
of my emotional energy to the church.

Clarity came for me one night over a fire in my backyard with my
friend John. He remained quiet as I vented, unloading my frustrations. After a while he just quietly said, "I don't think you're seeing
the situation clearly. I wonder if you need to step away for a while.
Perhaps the distance might bring some clarity." His words surprised
me, since I expected him to resonate with my take on things. But in
my heart I knew he was right. My vision was clouded and I was not
treating others rightly. I decided to take a sabbatical from the church,
both to renew my spirit and to provide some space for other leaders
to step forward with fresh vision and new voices.

During that sabbatical season of several months, I took many long
walks and pulled lots of weeds in my wife's garden. During these soli-
tary hours, I had numerous conversations in my head as I tried to cool
down from that intense experience. I was writing a book on Paul at
the time and many passages from his letters were running through
my mind. Not surprisingly, Paul's letters began to interpret my experience, posing tough questions about how I was relating to my ministry
partners. To the Galatian churches struggling to remain unified in the
midst of an intense challenge, he writes:

> For the whole law is summed up in a single commandment, "You
> shall love your neighbor as yourself." If, however, you bite and de-
> vour one another, take care that you are not consumed by one another.
> (Gal. 5:14–15)

He writes to the Corinthians:

> Do you not know that you as a community are the temple of God
> and that the Spirit of God dwells among you? If anyone destroys
> the temple of God, God will destroy that person; for the temple
> of God is holy, which is what you as a community are. (1 Cor.
> 3:16–17, my translation)

I pondered whether I was fostering relationships characterized by "biting and devouring," with the result that our community would sustain damage. And was I the agent of division in our community—God's holy temple—so that I was putting myself in a place of judgment?

I had already become convinced of a community-oriented reading of Romans, seeing Paul's statements about those with minds set on the flesh as those who are passing judgment and causing community stress:

> For those who live according to the flesh set their minds on the things of the flesh, but those who live according to the Spirit set their minds on the things of the Spirit. To set the mind on the flesh is death, but to set the mind on the Spirit is life and peace. For this reason the mind that is set on the flesh is hostile to God; it does not submit to God's law—indeed it cannot, and those who are in the flesh cannot please God. (Rom. 8:5–8)

I sat with the uncomfortable question of whether my mind was set on fleshly desires—a quest for control, to have the final say in the future direction of our community. Were my relationships with others and my approach to our community making me a person who was "hostile to God," not submitting "to God's law"?

That season of reflection bore rich fruit for me. I felt renewed and also experienced wonderful reconciliation with some dear friends. It also helped me to see that it is entirely possible to have godly goals in ministry while adopting postures toward others of frustration, anger, resentment, coercion, and even verbal violence. Pastoral ministry can be filled with destructive competition on church staffs and between pastors of different churches. I began to see that the sorts of issues we were facing were very similar to those that Paul addressed in his letters: communities struggling to figure out how to practically embody faithfulness to the God revealed in Jesus; competition between ministry partners; churches dealing with fractures along ethnic lines or that involve making judgments about lifestyle choices. Although I had long read Paul's letters as material from which to construct "Pauline theology," I had not engaged them to discern how they might inform pastoral ministry. So good

Reflecting on Paul as a Pastor

This book is the result of the intervening years of reflection on Paul's pastoral ministry, and it springs from the conviction that his letters are a gold mine of wisdom and insight for pastors. After all, a significant aspect of Paul's apostolic ministry involved a pastoral task. While Christians rightly read his letters as a resource for theology, Paul did not see himself as a professional theologian in the modern sense. He was more of a church planter, establishing churches around the Mediterranean world and then writing letters to give them counsel to resolve conflicts, rebuke them for mistreating one another, encourage them for their faithfulness, instruct them in living out the kingdom of God in their local situation, and to exhort them to continue on in the faith. Paul certainly drew upon his rich conception of the gospel and his profound theological grasp of the Scriptures of Israel in addressing them, but when we read Paul's letters we are not necessarily reading works of theology. We are encountering a theologically informed pastor counseling his churches in living into the fullness of the gospel. We find in Paul a counselor advising his communities as to how they might embody the resurrection life of God on earth.

Paul, however, pastored in a very different world from ours. We might expect there to be differences between Paul's world and ours given the distance of thousands of miles (I'm assuming most of my readers do not live near the Mediterranean Sea) and nearly two thousand years, but the differences are greater than that. Paul saw the world very differently and his imagination of how it all held together was informed by different sources and shaped by different forces from those that determine modern conceptions. It was a Scripture-saturated and Bible-shaped world, and his view of how it all worked was informed by his thorough knowledge of Scripture and Jewish tradition. The aim of this book is to reflect on how this affected Paul's pastoral approach.

This book is a theological, cultural, and pastoral reflection on the New Testament portrayal of Paul as a pastor with the aim of developing wisdom for contemporary church leaders. It is *theological* because I am writing as a Christian seeking to gain wisdom for living faithfully in the church of Jesus Christ. While I hope that what I say faithfully represents legitimate interpretive options in the eyes of biblical scholars, this is not a contribution to New Testament scholarship. I have very few footnotes and do not engage with the views of other scholars, from whom I have learned much. This is a book for pastors.

The book is also *cultural* in that I will be engaging the New Testament text alongside the dynamics, pressures, and tensions that shape contemporary pastoral ministry. I have learned much from several extended seasons of pastoral ministry and have enjoyed many conversations with ministry leaders in a variety of settings—women and men who serve in urban and rural churches and on several continents. Paul's letters have great wisdom to impart to pastors as they struggle with image maintenance and the expectations of others. He was familiar with "professional competition" and envy between fellow pastors and churches. Since he employed a social medium to communicate with his churches (i.e., letters), he understood the dynamics with which we struggle in an age dominated by social media. The discussions in the pages that follow, therefore, will bring contemporary pastoral dynamics into theological conversation with the letters of Paul and Luke's portrayal of Paul in Acts in order to provide wisdom for pastors and ministry practitioners.

And finally, as I just mentioned, this book is a *reflection* on the New Testament portrait of Paul as a pastor of his churches. There are legitimate historical-critical questions surrounding Paul's letters and how to assess Acts as a historical document, and other aspects of Paul's life, writings, and career are ripe for investigation. For my purposes in this book, however, I will focus on the New Testament portrait of Paul as we have it. The thirteen letters that bear his name portray him counseling and fostering the growth of the churches he planted. In addition, in the Book of Acts, Luke's account of the growth of the Jesus movement around the Mediterranean, we find an extended account of Paul's ministry—his violent opposition to the church, his dramatic reversal after encountering Jesus, his relationship with fellow ministry leaders, and his ongoing relationships with the churches. In the Pauline letters and what Luke writes of his ministry, then, we have a rich resource for reflecting on contemporary pastoral ministry. Four features characterize my approach.

Conversion of Paul's Ministry Imagination

First, I will reflect on the changes that took place in Paul's approach to ministry after his conversion. Now, that may sound a bit odd. Was Paul involved in ministry *before his conversion*? I express things this way because Paul's aims were nearly the same before his encounter with the Lord Jesus on the road to Damascus as they were afterward. Prior to his conversion, Paul was vigorously engaged in attempting to bring about resurrection life for God's people on earth. He was trying to move God to save Israel, ejecting the Romans from the land and initiating God's kingdom. This is how Pharisees would have understood "resurrection"—God fulfilling his promises to Israel, liberating them from their oppressors, pouring out the fullness of his restorative work on creation, and setting up his rule on earth with Israel prominently situated at the center of God's reign. Before his encounter with Christ, then, *Paul was consumed with the resurrection*. He certainly underwent dramatic changes after his transformation on the way to Damascus, but his agenda had always been oriented by resurrection. Paul's later apostolic commission involved founding and growing communities of resurrection life throughout the Mediterranean. It is just that for Paul *the manner* in which this would be brought about was dramatically different. This is what I mean when I write that Paul's ministry imagination underwent a thorough renovation. He had been "in ministry" before and after his conversion in that he was always trying to bring about God's aims for God's people.

We will explore these differences in order to understand how it is that pastors in our day can deal with temptations toward worldly and destructive forms of ministry. I assume that most, if not all, pastors want what is good for their churches; they desperately want to see God's aims brought about for God's people. But they can easily fall prey to the temptation of trying to bring those about through inappropriate means, ultimately undermining their efforts and generating dynamics of destruction. This creates intense frustration both in ministers and among the people they serve. My hope is that as we reflect on Paul's radical conversion of ministry mode we will discern how our own ministry practices and postures can be transformed and redeemed.

The Church's Cosmic Situation

According to Paul's conception of reality, the church is set within a cosmically contested situation. There is more wrong with the world and with all of reality than the mere fact that humans are sinners. According to Paul's inherited Jewish worldview stemming from the Scriptures of Israel, all of reality is far more messed up than most modern Christians realize. There is God's arch-enemy, Satan, who is at work in the world. There are cosmic ruler figures—the powers and authorities—who sow within human cultures perverted ideologies along with a bewildering array of available enslaving ways of life. And Paul sees other cosmic actors at work, personifying mysterious entities as having wills, aims, and intentions: Sin, Death, and Flesh.[1] All of these figures make up what we might call "the apocalyptic power alliance," a strikingly dramatic and wonderfully helpful way to describe how this collection of cosmic entities conspire to weave a brilliantly intricate matrix that makes up our current experience of life in a corrupted world.[2] These actors join in scheming to ensure that humanity does not experience God's order of flourishing in this world.

Paul understands the death of Christ as a triumph over these evil

1. Because Paul presents these personified agents as scheming against humanity to divide and destroy, a dynamic I describe further in chapter 4, I capitalize these terms throughout the book when I refer to them.

2. J. Christiaan Beker, *Paul the Apostle: The Triumph of God in Life and Thought* (Philadelphia: Fortress Press, 1980), 190.

cosmic powers. In Christ, God has broken their enslaving grip over creation and has begun to free his world from their malignant influence. At the future day of Christ, God will complete this work and fully restore creation, but the church is the initial phase of that work. The church, for Paul, is the presence of God in Christ by the Spirit, who delivers to the church the same power whereby God raised Jesus from the dead. These communities are outbreaks of the future kingdom of God, sites of resurrection life on earth, enlivened and animated by the Spirit, the life-giving presence of God.

These communities of God's resurrection-powered presence exist, however, in cosmically hostile territory. The present evil age persists, even as it goes down to destruction over the long and slow course of what we call "history." It seems that these evil powers—already defeated but not yet completely destroyed—are attempting to ruin as much of God's good world as they can before God annihilates them. Though their absolute grip on the world has been broken, they still do great damage. Churches, therefore, feel the tug and pull of being in a cosmic situation where two ages are up and running. The new age has been initiated by God in the death and resurrection of Christ, but the old age persists, even though God dealt it a fatal blow at the death of Christ and the sending of the Spirit into enemy territory.

This cosmic scenario informs much of Paul's counsel to his churches and it shapes how he discerns community conflicts. Where there are factions or where groups assert their rights over others, Paul discerns behaviors that stir up and activate destructive cosmic dynamics within the community. Such postures and patterns of community life are not just "unfortunate." They insinuate satanic dynamics into a community; they assert the rule of the fallen powers that work for the destruction of the community. Alternatively, when a community is characterized by self-giving love and service, Paul sees the Spirit at work to bear gospel fruit and frustrate the powers of darkness. And he exhorts all his communities to act in such ways that will stir up and activate the presence of the Holy Spirit to enable the powers of renewal, restoration, and redemption to overtake and redeem communities.

Paul envisions the church, therefore, as situated within a cosmically contested environment. That is, the church occupies a space within the cosmos in which hostile forces work to undermine and destroy God's intentions. If pastors are not alert to these, they will not grasp the cosmically destructive power of certain modes of ministry. They will also fail to discern the spiritual dynamics in play in various situations. These forces play very specific roles in the drama of church life, and Paul makes mention of them throughout his letters and in his counsel to his churches. Most modern ministry practitioners conceive of church life in a straightforward manner without taking into account these forces. I hope that the discussions in these pages help pastors become alert to the cosmic and spiritual dynamics in play so that they can understand the character of their approaches to ministry and discern how to proceed in situations of opportunity, conflict, and challenge.

The Church as the Site of Resurrection Presence on Earth

A third contribution of this book for coming to grips with pastoral ministry, related to the previous point, is to understand the church as the place on earth where God resides. The church is not at all an organization *of this world* and it cannot be conceived of in that way. Ministry practitioners may fall into the trap of envisioning the church as if it were an organization that can be led the way a CEO leads a company, the way a manager leads a business or the way a general leads an army. But the church is utterly unique—the only body of people on earth within whom God dwells. And he is not just among us in a general sense. God is present in the church in power, radiating resurrection life by his Spirit. It is the power of the resurrection that dwells among us, God's life-giving presence that renews, redeems, nourishes, and sustains us. The very power that raised Jesus from the dead now fills and pervades churches that gather in the name of Jesus. This reality shapes Paul's outlook, too, and we'll see how his instructions are aimed at having his churches stir up, activate, and increase that life-generating presence.

This reality is significant because it determines Paul's exhortations. Paul appeals to his communities to conduct themselves in certain ways not merely because these fit a "Christian ethic," or because they seem right. He commends attitudes and behaviors that activate and increase God's resurrection presence among them. There are patterns of life that draw upon and stir up God's life-giving power so that people are renewed, conflicts are resolved, broken hearts are restored, and the community is made to flourish. Paul's apostolic ministry involved planting churches that were communities of resurrection life—experiences of resurrection presence in anticipation of the full realization of resurrection in the future. That meant that pastoral ministry for Paul entailed fostering communities of resurrection life, helping churches come to understand how they can experience the power of God's resurrection presence within them.

The New Testament Portrait of Paul as Pastor

A fourth contribution of this book is that it goes beyond mining the "Pastoral Letters" (1 and 2 Timothy, Titus) to reflect theologically on the entire New Testament portrait of Paul, including the Book of Acts. It would indeed be valuable to focus on the Pastoral Letters, for much can be gained by doing so. But I have decided to read all of Paul's letters as informing his pastoral approach since it is in the more "theological letters," such as Romans, the Corinthian letters, and Galatians, that we actually see Paul doing the work of pastoral ministry. He is not writing theological works for their own sake but resolving conflicts and pointing the way toward faithfully and creatively embodying as communities the resurrection realities of the kingdom of God. We can, therefore, sit alongside all of his letters and observe Paul the pastor in action. How does he discern conflict? What frames of thought does he use to conceive of ministry partnerships? How does he think about conflict theologically and recommend resolutions?

Of course, there are some unique aspects of Paul's ministry that do not transfer to the rest of us. He was one of a small number of apostles and he alone was sent to preach the gospel to the nations. But like many others in our day, he planted churches, pastoring them in his letters. He states that he would far rather be present with the churches to which he writes, but because this was impossible, he needed to write letters. While that was unfortunate for him, it is a great help to us because in his letters we can observe Paul's pastoral practice in action. This has the promise of helping us discern how we can fruitfully and faithfully envision our pastoral ministries today.

1

Paul's Unconverted Ministry

Pastors struggle with anger and frustration. Leading a church is hard work and it is easy to lose patience with God's people. At the same time, pastors love what they do, serving God and genuinely caring for the people in their churches. And, of course, they do not want to appear abrasive or condescending, or to fall into ordering people around, so they rarely find outlets for dealing with slights, criticisms, personality conflicts, and other disappointments.

I knew a pastor whom I will call "Kevin" who had become frustrated with his church and with his small support staff. When he was younger he was part of a vibrant church in a major city that was led by a dynamic preacher with a magnetic personality. The pastoral staff was large and the church had no shortage of resources to send them to conferences and to offer many other professional development opportunities. His experience at this big, "successful" church shaped his conceptions of his future ministry. He later became the lone pastor of a small church in a less populated area of the country that had far fewer resources. He nurtured ambitions about leading the congregation toward experiencing the sort of thriving community life that characterized his former church.

Over a few years, however, very little had changed and Kevin grew frustrated. He harbored a desire for the church to be a dynamic community of blessing, to reach into the community with vigor, and to experience growth in its various ministries. Because Kevin had formerly enjoyed plenty of professional development opportunities, he began to grow resentful that he could no longer go to conferences and catch up with pastoral colleagues as he once did.

Kevin's preaching began to have an edge to it. People began to feel that he was berating the congregation in his Sunday sermons. Some of the church staff felt that he was being short with them. In Kevin's view, they were becoming obstacles, not committed to ministry as they should be, failing to live into the vision he felt God had set for them. He often complained about his situation to former ministry partners at his previous church, claiming that his leaders were getting in the way of where he wanted to "take the church." He was discouraged that they were not getting on board with his vision the way he wanted them to. He began to see many of the people in his church as problems to be solved. He grew bitter, frustrated, impatient, and angry. One Sunday a lay leader took him aside and mentioned that he seemed sullen and irritated. Word had spread that he had recently blown up at the youth pastor. Leaders in the church were doing what they could to avoid being around him.

This sort of situation is far more common than many would expect. It is surprisingly easy to slip into a mode of ministry where we are trying to bring about God's blessings in a destructively forceful or coercive manner. From our perspective, of course, we are only trying to carry out God's calling for us. After all, most pastors want their communities to be life-giving havens where people experience the power and presence of God. We may attempt, however, to get there in ways that counteract our intentions. Pastors in situations like this require a conversion of their ministry imaginations.[1] Their entire outlook must be transformed regarding their postures toward their churches, toward their ministry partners, and toward the manner in which God works among them.

Such a conversion took place in Paul's life. In this chapter, and in the next two, we will reflect on the conversion of Paul's pastoral

---

1. I am adapting this expression from the title of a volume of essays by Richard Hays (*The Conversion of the Imagination: Paul as Interpreter of Israel's Scripture* [Grand Rapids: Eerdmans, 2005]).

imagination that occurred after his dramatic encounter with the exalted Lord Jesus on the road to Damascus. That encounter thoroughly changed Paul's life, his mode of ministry, and his vision of how God works in the world.

Paul's Pre-Christian Pursuit of Resurrection

Paul had been trained as a Pharisee and remained one throughout his life.[2] Luke mentions that the Pharisees believed in the resurrection, whereas the Sadducees did not (Acts 23:8). We might read this as if the Pharisees had a doctrinal statement buried in a desk somewhere back at Pharisaic headquarters with a line item indicating their belief in the resurrection. But this assumption underestimates the significance of the resurrection for them. The resurrection was the singular impulse that united the Pharisees and drove their agenda. It oriented all their activities and dominated their study, their teaching, and their praying. They longed for the resurrection, praying for it throughout the day and tirelessly working to bring it about.[3]

Their conception of the resurrection did not merely mean that at the great day of the Lord each righteous individual would be raised from the dead. It involved that and so much more. It had to do with the restoration of God's purposes and the fulfillment of all of God's promises to God's people. Along with all other Jews, the Pharisees felt keenly the tragedy that God's purposes were not being worked out in the world the way they should be. God had intended for Israel to be his special possession, to enjoy his blessing, and to be the people on

2. Paul remained a Pharisee after his conversion. In his defense before the Jerusalem council, late in his apostolic career, he cried out, "Brothers, I am a Pharisee, a son of Pharisees. I am on trial concerning the hope of the resurrection of the dead" (Acts 23:6). He was one of a large number of priests and Pharisees who became obedient to the faith during the early decades of the church (Acts 6:7; 15:5; 21:20).

3. For a discussion of the Pharisees' hopes for resurrection that drove their agenda, see N. T. Wright, *What Saint Paul Really Said: Was Paul of Tarsus the Real Founder of Christianity?* (Grand Rapids: Eerdmans, 1997), 25–35.

earth among whom his glory was clearly seen. They were supposed to joyfully inhabit the kingdom of God on earth by experiencing the fullness of God's *shalom*, which meant a flourishing economy, with each family owning land and living off its plenty. And they were to enjoy the worship of the one true God at the temple in Jerusalem, overseen by godly priests under the authority of uncompromised leaders. Thus enjoying God's restored rule, Israel was to lead the nations of the world in the worship of the one true God.

But none of this was a reality. First-century Jews lived under the oppressive rule of an occupying force—the pagan Romans. They were beaten down and mistreated and faced the hopeless reality of crushing poverty. Their national leaders were compromised by alliances with the Romans that allowed them to hold on to their positions. The tangled web of power interests fed a system of oppression that felt worlds away from God's intended national order of flourishing. Along with other Jews, Pharisees longed for the fulfillment of the promises of God to liberate them, to purify their land, and to restore his gracious reign.

Resurrection, to the Pharisees, indicated this larger, national scenario of economic, political, and religious restoration of God's promises to the patriarchs and to Israel through the prophets. Resurrection referred to the reality of God pouring out his life-giving presence upon the land and the holistic renewal of Israel's national life—the restoration of flourishing at every level of society. Resurrection would transform the entire tragic situation facing the nation. The God of all creation would return to Zion and demonstrate that Israel was indeed his people by driving out the Romans and removing the stain of their impurity. Hearts would be satisfied and lives would be renewed. God would exalt the righteous and destroy the wicked. In this restored order, Israel would then begin to lead the nations, instructing them to obey the God of Israel and directing them in the worship of the one true God.

Before his conversion, then, Paul was desperate for God's people to experience resurrection—the restoration of God's gracious reign among them. He was convinced that he and his Pharisaic associates were the key to the God of Israel unleashing this holistic salvation program on the nation. This passionate conviction involved him in a daily pursuit of trying to move God to save Israel.

Paul's Ministry Mode of Coercive Power

I refer to Paul's preconversion conduct as a mode of "ministry" because that is how he would have seen it. He was serving God, convinced that God would initiate resurrection when Israel became a people of faithful Torah observance uncompromised by the cultural influences of paganism. When Israel became sufficiently obedient, God would judge the wicked, purify the land of the defiling presence of the pagan Romans, and pour out salvation on the nation. This hope drove Paul and his ministry associates to seek to present to God a nation faithfully obedient to their conception of Scripture. They reasoned that if God had sent Israel into exile because of unfaithfulness to the Torah, then surely the nation's renewed faithfulness would move him to bring about restoration.

This outlook, based on Scriptural reasoning, led to a ministry mode of coercive power, and even violence. Paul believed that the main obstacle to salvation was the presence of sinners among God's people. God would restore Israel and drive the Romans from the land were it not for the many Jews whose faithfulness to Torah was questionable, half-hearted, or inconsistent. The Pharisees were meticulously attentive to a form of purity in daily life that matched the Torah's instructions for priests in their rituals within the temple. And they taught Jewish commoners to carry out these same practices. The presence of Jews who were either unconcerned or inconsistent in their view was a grief and tremendous frustration. These people were standing in the way of God saving Israel and transforming their oppressed land into the glorious kingdom of God.

Paul describes himself as surpassing his contemporaries with regard to zeal (Gal. 1:14), which he displayed by passionately pursuing the purity of the Jewish people from the stain of foreign cultural influences. Not only did he teach and exhort Jews toward a careful faithfulness to God and to his understanding of the Mosaic law, but he demonstrated a zeal that involved persecution, which we see in his encounter with the early followers of Jesus.

Scripture does not indicate whether or not Paul ever encountered Jesus during his earthly ministry. He may have been one of those who went out to question Jesus in order to find out more about him (cf. Mark 7:1). It is a fascinating exercise to imagine Paul's response to Jesus, if indeed he knew of him. The land of Israel/Palestine is not a huge place and word about various teachers got around quickly, especially among those who were looking out for indications of God's coming salvation. Was he intrigued? Was he hopeful that Jesus was indeed the Messiah of Israel's God? On the other hand, he may have been one of those who quickly opposed Jesus. Whatever the case, certainly after Jesus's death Paul became an intense persecutor of the followers of Jesus. But why did he do this? What drove Paul to attempt to stamp out the early Christian movement?

Paul saw clearly that God had rendered his judgment of Jesus by how he was killed. Jesus had been put to death on a cross, and Paul knew well what was written in the Torah:

> When someone is convicted of a crime punishable by death and is executed, and you hang him on a tree, his corpse must not remain all night upon the tree; you shall bury him that same day, *for anyone hung on a tree is under God's curse.* You must not defile the land that the Lord your God is giving you for possession. (Deut. 21:22–23)

For Paul, Torah clearly expressed God's judgment regarding Jesus. He had been hung on a tree and was therefore cursed of God. Paul viewed the followers of Jesus who were claiming otherwise as idolatrous sinners since they were worshiping a person God had condemned, defiantly rejecting God's verdict on this messianic pretender. Paul saw these early Jewish Christians as a stain on the land of Israel and an affront to God. They were unfaithful Israelites who were preventing God from saving the nation, keeping him from pouring out resurrection life on earth. For Paul, these Jesus-followers needed to be stopped by any means necessary.

It is crucial to recognize that it was Paul's passion for resurrection—for God's salvation—that drove him to try to stamp out the church, and this led him to a program of coercive power and violence. According to Paul's later ministry partner, Luke, Paul was present at the killing of Stephen and approved of what was done (Acts 7:58–8:1). After this he led an initiative against the followers of Jesus:

> That day a severe persecution began against the church in Jerusalem, and all except the apostles were scattered throughout the countryside of Judea and Samaria. Devout men buried Stephen and made loud lamentation over him. But Saul was ravaging the church by entering house after house; dragging off both men and women, he committed them to prison. (Acts 8:1–3)

Just prior to his encounter with the exalted Lord Jesus, Luke describes how Paul,

> still breathing threats and murder against the disciples of the Lord, went to the high priest and asked him for letters to the synagogues at Damascus, so that if he found any who belonged to the Way, men or women, he might bring them bound to Jerusalem. (Acts 9:1–2)

In a later reflection on his life and career, Paul notes that he had been a "blasphemer" and "violent aggressor" (1 Tim. 1:13). When he speaks of "blasphemy," Paul may be referring to the way he had formerly talked about Jesus whom he later regarded as the Messiah. But it may also be that his reference to blasphemy recalled his violent and condemnatory speech about Christians. The Greek term for "blasphemy" refers to abusive or reviling speech that can be directed toward other people or against God. While Paul may or may not have spoken blasphemously about Jesus before his conversion, he was undoubtedly engaged in a program of verbal and physical violence against his followers.

Keep in mind that in all of this, zeal for God and God's glory drove Paul. He longed to see God's word enacted by God's people. In his mind his motivations were pure! He wanted Israel to enjoy the fullness of resurrection life—the life of God on earth that would bring about renewal, restoration, and the completion of redemption. But Paul was seeking this through power. He was coercive toward others and had adopted postures of domination and threat. He had become verbally abusive and violent.

Pastors and church leaders can fall into this very same trap. They genuinely love the congregations they serve and desire for God to be exalted in their churches. They feel they have a vision for what their church could be and the ways their church could serve. They want to see their communities characterized by joy as they embody being God's new family. They may be disappointed when they see little fruit and slow growth. Ministry leaders can grow frustrated by their churches and demonstrate postures of coercive power, manipulation, and verbal violence toward the people they are called to serve.

I have witnessed on more than one occasion a pastor scolding a congregation for failing to measure up to expectations or for lacking a passion for God's purposes. I have heard passive-aggressive comments from the pulpit about what pastors perceive as their church's lack of commitment. Perhaps it is a special ministry effort that the pastor had been excited about or a drive to raise money about which the pastor had great expectations. Unfulfilled hopes generated a scolding posture from the pastor. It is not far from the mark to call this verbal violence. Like Paul "breathing out threats," pastors can grow so frustrated that they berate their staff or lay ministry leaders for not meeting expectations. In the midst of ministry disappointments and setbacks, pastors are tempted to adopt a ministry mode that resembles Paul's preconversion pursuit of resurrection. It is tempting to imagine that sheer force can bring about God's blessing.

Paul Pursued a Personal Identity of Power

Paul's desire to bring about resurrection realities at the national level was matched by his attempt to establish a basis for making his own claim for salvation at the day of the Lord based on the construction of a socially approved identity. That is, Paul assumed that on the day that God saved Israel by pouring out resurrection, God would vindicate him on the basis of who he had become in the eyes of others. He had worked very hard to establish an identity oriented by a certain kind of Torah observance and faithfulness to the traditions he had inherited. He figured that the impressive social status he had cultivated in his zealous pursuits would gain him the verdict of "righteous" from the God of Israel at the day of judgment. God would gladly approve of his efforts in seeking to foster a passion for righteousness among his fellow Israelites.

At the day of the Lord, Paul wanted to be exalted by the God of Israel. He wanted to hear "well done, good and faithful servant." He had equated the praise of men with the anticipated praise of God. He was respected and admired by his peers, and many others thought highly of him, based on his knowledge of Scripture, his passion for the purity of Israel, and his clear articulation of how the glory of God ought to be embodied in everyday life. Paul was confident that at the final judgment God would vindicate him as someone at the very center of God's people, a leader of God's chosen ones, a teacher of Israel.

In Philippians 3, Paul reflects on his former pursuit of accumulating credentials to build a powerful personal identity in the hopes of establishing a claim to righteousness before God. He had formerly put confidence "in the flesh"—that is, in his impressive resume:

> If anyone else has reason to be confident in the flesh, I have more: circumcised on the eighth day, a member of the people of Israel, of the tribe of Benjamin, a Hebrew born of Hebrews; as to the law, a Pharisee; as to zeal, a persecutor of the church; as to righteousness under the law, blameless. (Phil. 3:4–6)

The "confidence" that Paul refers to has to do with his expectation that he would personally participate in the resurrection (v. 11). The goal toward which he had directed his entire life was to be counted among the righteous who would be claimed by God at the day of the Lord and welcomed into eternal life. This remained his goal after his conversion, though he had come to see that there was a radically different basis for this taking place. We will explore that in the next few chapters.

Paul had formerly placed full confidence in his inherited credentials and in his lifetime pursuit of a constructed social identity based on the central elements of his Jewish heritage. He was the son of faithful Jewish parents, a genuine Israelite, and trained as a Pharisee, with careful and meticulous observance of the Mosaic law according to his inherited traditions. He demonstrated his zeal for the purity of God's people by persecuting the movement that was preventing God from saving Israel—the church. Further, Paul says that he was blameless regarding the righteousness of the law (v. 6). He has in mind here his faithful adherence to the inherited standards and traditions regarding how to observe Torah.

Just as any religious subculture has expectations and guidelines for behavior stemming from their interpretation of Scripture, the Pharisees had theirs. Such groups, of course, do not think that their standards are in any sense distinct from Torah. They imagine that they have captured the specific ways that Scripture should be obeyed. According to the complex set of expectations that constituted this way of life, Paul was blameless. He was faithful to Torah as he and his community understood it.

The social approval Paul received based on this life of conformity to cultural expectations shaped his identity. He was an approved, exalted, and respected person. He was faithful to Torah, and he was certain that this is how the God of Israel would have seen him. There was no doubt in his mind that when the day of the Lord arrived, Paul would be counted among the righteous!

The desire to pursue a social status determined by cultural expectations affects contemporary ministry practitioners, as well. We live

in an era where pastoral ministry is no longer seen in terms of being a *unfortunate*
"shepherd," which is what "pastor" means. A shepherd in the ancient
world was one of the lowest and least socially approved vocations. It
is basically what you did when you could do no other sort of task. In
our day, however, pastoral identity is often constructed in terms of
a business executive, someone who is respected in the community
for their decisive leadership, their administrative skill, their vision-
casting, and their ability to get things done. This puts pressure on
pastors to quest after credentials in order to appear capable, competent, and accomplished.

From one perspective, the proliferation and popularity of Doctor
of Ministry programs in the last quarter of the twentieth century was
driven by the hunger among pastors for a credential that would boost
their image of competence and prestige. In some denominational circles, leaders are referred to by their title of "Dr.," which plants the
desire in the hearts of young ministers to aspire to likewise being
addressed as "doctor" one day. And in some churches, pastors insist
on being called "doctor," perhaps because they feel that this is more
prestigious and respectable than being addressed as "pastor," or just
being called by their first name.

Much critical material has been written about Doctor of Ministry
degrees, and I do not intend to add to the critiques.[4] Further, I do
realize that seminary training toward a degree may be useful to gain
necessary skills for serving God's people. I only intend to highlight
here that seeking a credential in order to construct an identity that
seems to have meaning in an effort to be lifted up above others in the
church is the same pursuit that formerly consumed Paul. As we will
see in the next chapter, Paul rejected this approach to constructing his
identity and saw it not only as useless, but as an obstacle to genuine
identity in Christ.

4. David F. Wells, "The D-Min-Ization of the Ministry" in *No God but
God: Breaking with the Idols of Our Age*, Os Guinness and John Seel, eds.
(Chicago: Moody Press, 1992). See also Wells's *No Place for Truth, or, Whatever Happened to Evangelical Theology* (Grand Rapids: Eerdmans, 1993),
218–57.

Paul's Spirit of Competition with Ministry Partners

This pursuit of achieving ever-higher social status and increased credentials put Paul in competition with his ministry partners. He reflects this competitive spirit in his comments in Philippians 3:4 that
he had more reason than anyone else to put confidence in the flesh.
In Galatians 1:14, he notes that he "advanced in Judaism beyond many
among my people of the same age, for I was far more zealous for the
traditions of my ancestors." In speaking of "Judaism," Paul does not
mean merely the religion we know as Judaism in our day, but the
specific movement among Jews characterized by zeal for the purity
of God's people and resistance to any sort of Hellenistic cultural influence. Even among this passionate group that was committed to pu-
rifying God's people from foreign corruption, Paul was outstripping
them all in activist zeal.

In 2 Corinthians 10:12, Paul speaks about the folly of comparing
 ministries and ministry skillfulness, indicating that he was indeed
aware of the reality that among ministry practitioners a spirit of competition can not only be present, but thrive. Further, Paul says quite
a bit about ambition in his letters, contrasting godly ambition with
corrupted ambition in Romans 2:7–10. He also warns against doing
anything from selfish ambition in Philippians 2:3, leading into a theologically powerful discussion of the alternative way of Jesus (vv. 5–11).
At the beginning of his letter to the Philippians, he notes that some
were preaching Christ from selfish ambition (1:17). I wonder if Paul
had so much to say about this topic because he was well-acquainted
with overpowering personal ambition. Not only was he part of the
group seeking the purity of Israel, but he was consciously agitating
to outpace his contemporaries in zeal. It is certainly instructive that
when Paul looks back on his life before he was an apostle of Jesus
Christ, he could easily point to his former spirit of competition.

Ordinary Christians may be surprised to discover that professional jealousy is alive and well among the ranks of pastors and ministry practitioners. I have spoken with many pastors who served on
church staffs that were characterized by a competitive spirit. In one

instance, the senior pastor of a church had announced he was going to retire within a few months. This ignited a range of destructive
dynamics and mutual suspicion rooted in a spirit of competition
between staff pastors who were agitating to be considered for the
soon-to-be-vacant position.

In another instance, the popularity of a staff pastor's Bible study
made his fellow pastors jealous. Within a year, this person's ministry
partners had convinced the senior pastor and lay leaders that this
popular pastor was not a "team player," and a few months later he
was forced to resign.

Doing ministry in an era that has professionalized the pastorate
creates a number of destructive dynamics. Pastors and ministry leaders are tempted to find their significance and identity in the size of
their church or the success of the ministry they oversee. In situations
like these, the temptation will always be present to adopt a spirit
of competition with pastors of other churches or with others on a
church staff. Not only this, but entire churches can look on churches
across town with envy and jealousy if that fellowship enjoys a season of numerical growth, or if a "rival" ministry is pursuing exciting
initiatives.

Paul's Tribal Commitments

As we just noted, Paul had surpassed his contemporaries in zeal "for
the traditions of [his] ancestors" (Gal. 1:14). He conspicuously does
not say that he was formerly zealous for *Scripture* or for *God*. Paul
likely would have characterized his former life as he had described
his fellow Jews who were not Jesus-followers in Romans 10:2 as those
who have a zeal for God, but one that is not enlightened. What he
thought was zeal for God turned out to be passion for tradition, for
his own ideological tribe. Paul's experience reveals the possibility of
mistaking loyalty to human traditions or commitment to group identity for allegiance to the one true God. And we can be sure that the
traditions to which Paul was committed were originally developed
to help interpret Scripture and to shed light on how all aspects of life

could enjoy the blessing of God. Over time, however, such commitments take on lives of their own, and adherents to a tradition begin to associate their way of thinking and acting with Scripture itself. Paul was convinced that because he was loyal to his inherited framework of thought and set of practices that he was clearly pleasing the God of Israel. He discovered, however, that his passion had put him in a position of opposition to God, attempting to destroy the work that God was building.

We see the same dynamics taking place in our day. We may mistake our membership in a denomination or commitment to a theological tradition for loyalty to Christ. A clear sign of this happening is when our group compares itself with other traditions and claims superior faithfulness. Protestants may be certain they are advancing the purity of Scripture as they critique Roman Catholics. Baptists may convince themselves that Presbyterians misinterpret Scripture and so must oppose them. When I was in seminary, we spent much of our time criticizing other evangelical traditions so that we were far more aware of those differences than we were familiar with Scripture.

Many observers of evangelical culture have noted the "tribalization" of evangelicalism. What was once a renewal movement within mainline denominations became a collection of separatist groups that justified their existence by claims of biblical fidelity and accusations that denominations and other groups were unfaithful. They became most vociferous toward groups that closely resembled them with regard to theological vision and ministry practice, overemphasizing their differences with others. In addition, because group cohesion is fostered by criticism of others, when group members speak constructively or sympathetically of rival groups, they are viewed with suspicion. Perhaps such people lack faithfulness! Many people feel they need to choose sides in these battles, or pitch their tent with this or that tradition.

Many ministry fellowships and denominations develop out of desires to provide resources, to encourage and strengthen weary pastors, and to sustain the faithful ministries of pastors in local churches. Soon enough, however, such organizations can develop the sort of destructive group identity that views outsiders with suspicion.

Denominational identity has been declining in America over the last few decades, but we should not imagine that group identity is no longer important. It has simply shifted. Many pastors now identify with one or another of many parachurch organizations designed to serve and further equip ministry practitioners. While the founding of such groups is well-motivated, the same dynamics of group identity and zeal for faithfulness to a certain interpretation of the Christian faith are often recreated.

One way this group loyalty shows up is in identification with a well-known figure, a celebrity pastor. As a pastor gains prominence and his or her "platform" expands, a following develops and ministry practitioners begin to identify themselves and their churches with that figure. They organize their ministries according to the materials produced and books published by the celebrity figure, and interpret challenges and opportunities in terms supplied by these resources. They may even borrow significant material from their books or sermons and begin to sound just like the person they admire.

A destructive tribalism is developing when we find ourselves minimizing others, criticizing them regularly or even attacking them out of loyalty to one person, organization, school of thought or theological tradition. We should be alert to the temptation to construct a ministry identity according to any individual or ministry organization.

⚡ For Paul, Image Was Everything

We live in a culture oriented toward image maintenance. While publicists and marketers have tried to influence popular opinion for decades, the dynamics of controlling others' perception of us are now pervasive because of social media. Through our pictures, online updates, and noting the activities, movies, bands, and shows we like, we present to the world our desired image of ourselves. Paul was familiar with these dynamics and in his pre-Christian days was wrapped up in them. He demonstrates a keen awareness of the pressures of perception and how information can be manipulated to create and portray a projected image to others.

We will discuss 2 Corinthians 12:6 in greater detail in another chapter, so I will just point to it for now. In this text, Paul states that he does not want to report to the Corinthians his supernatural experiences "so that no one may think better of me than what is seen in me or heard from me." That is, they know him from a distance and so they may be tempted to think he is more impressive and exalted than he really is, or that he is more spiritual, godly, and competent than he really is.

This is a remarkable statement that runs directly against the grain of an orientation toward image cultivation, but it demonstrates that Paul was familiar with the dynamics of perception-management because it was such a significant part of his previous ministry mode. This makes sense in light of his lifelong pursuit of credentials that would improve his social status. In his former life, he was trying to please people (Gal. 1:10), even though, as we indicated previously, Paul would not have recognized that this was what he was doing. Very often our own motives are hidden from us. Only in light of God laying us bare—our being known by God—do our inner motivations become exposed to us.

Image maintenance involves an intentional cultivation of a projected self in an effort to create impressions and perceptions in others. We construct and maintain an inauthentic public identity in order to please others, impress them, or change their impression. Because an image is constructed and inauthentic, it is extremely exhausting. If I am engaged in this effort, I cannot afford to be honest or vulnerable. I cannot respond authentically lest I inadvertently let others in on the truth. Image maintenance involves at least the following dynamics.

First, when I am trying to project an image, I am intensely attentive to controlling how I am perceived, or how others think about me. I am committed to shaping others' opinions and impressions of me because their evaluation of me is so crucial. I will do whatever it takes to make them impressed with me or to make them happy. This makes me vulnerable to compromise. I will feel immense pressure to let go of dearly held beliefs and convictions because I may perceive that living by them will disappoint or upset others.

You can already tell how disastrous such an orientation is for pastors and church leaders. Such a person cannot be trusted to be faithful and true to her or his word. No matter what they say they believe, they will bend in the direction of popular opinion, or toward what they feel will make others happy.

Second, if I am oriented toward image maintenance, I will be more focused on managing others' perception of me than on the substance of who I am. That is, I won't be so concerned with being honest with others, seeking reconciliation, speaking plainly, and seeking to do what is right. I will focus on how others perceive me in ministry. I will hope to create the right impression. Matters of style will trump matters of substance.

I was part of a ministry staff at a large church a few decades ago and our weekly discussions were largely taken up with making sure the service went just so. We felt the need to create the right impression. The lighting had to be perfect; transitions in the service had to be seamless. When we thought about a certain person for a staff position, we were focused on how well they cultivated their public presentation. We would be horrified to think we were talking about stylish matters over substance, but we were. Looking back, we spoke far less about character than administrative skill and personal presentation.

Third, in certain situations pastors and ministry leaders may feel that they cannot display any uncertainty about the rightness of their cause, their course of action, or certain decisions that have been made. To show any doubt or hesitation is weakness. Staff members may feel pressured to present a "united front" when a difficult decision has been made, revealing no hesitation at all when others inquire.

Fourth, pastors may feel that they cannot be vulnerable about their own shortcomings, frailties or weaknesses. Certainly Paul would have felt this way. Pursuing the accumulation of credentials indicates living in such ways as to impress others and increase in social status and honor. This is easy to spot when it comes to celebrity pastors, but

ministry practitioners at every level face the same struggles. I know
a pastor who insulates himself from church members in an effort to
protect his image. He has a staff of pastors to handle the daily needs of
people in his church. His fear of disappointing parishioners who have
exalted expectations of him has driven him to avoid being known for
who he truly is.

Paul's Agenda Was More Important than People

Before his conversion, Paul's ministry agenda was to bring about
God's blessing on Israel and to produce resurrection life on a national scale. He was attempting to move God to act and to coerce
God's people toward the adoption of a more faithful mode of Torah
practice, as he saw it. He was also attempting to stake his own claim
to resurrection on the day of salvation. His vision for the nation and
for himself drove his treatment of others. It made him manipulative,
coercive, and violent, generating anger and frustration in him and in
others. This same dynamic can develop in contemporary ministry
situations when a pastor's vision for the church becomes the driving
force. I once heard a prominent pastor telling young ministry leaders
that the most important thing to have when they arrive at a church is
a vision for their ministry. He called on them to develop ambitious
goals for growth and for "ministry impact," claiming that "dreaming
big" demonstrated great faith in God.

In my experience, framing pastoral ministry in this way can have
negative consequences. It is quite possible that such ministry rhetoric
masks ungodly motivations. We can talk about how we want God to
do big things but it just may be that we desire the sort of impressive
ministry that will make us look good. Motivations are difficult to discern and desiring a growing church may stem from personal pride.
If my ministry is seen as "successful," it reflects well on my skills, my
giftedness, my value, and my godliness. We may not explicitly admit
this, but we can nurture these desires and conceal them with humble-
sounding clichés, like: "It's the Lord, not me."

Further, conceiving of a ministry vision before I get to know a community puts my dreams ahead of the health of the community I am serving. What if my dreams and plans need adjusting? What if they do not match the character of the community I am called to serve? I need to be extremely sensitive to the church I am serving to understand their history, their tragedies and pains, their joys and triumphs. Imposing a predetermined conception of what they need and how I am going to produce that does not manifest boldness or strong faith in God. It demonstrates a failure of love, compassion, and pastoral care. It is a refusal to participate in the surprising work of God as he slowly and lovingly moves within a community in ways that no one could predict.

I sat down with an old friend once to catch up and hear about his ministry. He is an impressive person with loads of charisma, the kind who can get to know anyone and seems to feel equally at ease talking to famous people and wait-staff in restaurants. I wondered if I would hear about his big plans for his ministry. I was surprised, however, when he told me about the rough time his community was enduring and that the people to whom he was ministering were worn out. He told me that his church was filled with people who had experienced trauma and just needed to gather and to find rest. He spoke about how he was focused on rehearsing with them God's overpowering grace and love. That is a pastor who knows his church's history and has avoided putting his vision before their needs.

When I make the mistake of putting my vision ahead of people, it makes me treat them as the means to meeting my goal. Faithful ministers, however, do not use people for their own purposes. People themselves—and their flourishing in Christ together as a community—are the goal of ministry and never the means to something else. If I view people as the means to producing my vision, I will treat them as expendable if they do not seem that they will get me where I want to go. I may see unremarkable people as not very useful. I will look for outwardly impressive people who can make a good immediate impression, those who can help generate buzz, but who may or may not have genuine Christian character, and who may do real damage to others.

This sort of growth conception of ministry has much in common with the economic ideology of capitalism. On this outlook, things are going well in the church if the numbers are increasing. People in the church (pastors, members, leaders) are like stockholders and pastors only want to report good news to them. Ministry leaders want to inform "investors" that their "investments" in the church are paying off. Stakeholders want growth, and they will feel good about the ministry and they will attach themselves to it when things are exciting and growing. In the New Testament, however, the main metaphor for the church is a family.[5] The church is made up of siblings in Jesus who are vitally connected to each other, and no one gets to choose their family. And in a family, no one is expendable. Prospects for growth may or may not be great, but what matters is that everyone looks after everyone else. What is crucial is the regular celebration of the bonds of family unity through meals and social gatherings to revisit and rehearse the new identity that God has given to us.

As parents know, having children involves getting to know strangers, people who turn out in ways we cannot predict and cannot program. Joyful families are those that clear space for everyone to develop and flourish, offering them freedom to grow and to become who they are in a loving community of affirmation, warmth, and wisdom. The same is true of the church. Pre-programmed expectations stifle freedom and demonstrate a failure to clear space for growth.

I once had a conversation with a pastor who was struggling with how to communicate to a certain person that she did not "belong" in their ministry. She was drawn to the fellowship of the community and wanted to be involved, but she did not fit the ministry profile, did not match the demographic they were trying to reach. What an awful thing when people are drawn to the church because they find life and warmth and acceptance, only to be told that they do not fit the profile and need to move on. God is the one who forms his church and builds his new family. We do not get to pick and choose who this will be.

5. Joseph H. Hellerman, *When the Church Was a Family: Recapturing Jesus' Vision for Authentic Christian Community* (Nashville: B&H Academic, 2009).

God develops his family—the church—out of unpredictable people. God calls us to love, welcome, and serve those who come our way.

Finally, this approach to ministry inflicts damage on a pastoral staff. Pastors are not CEOs of a business but members of the church family. They are also undergoing redemption. They, too, are being shaped by God in the midst of the community's journey through life. They are not experts who come to town, implement a plan, and get amazing results. Just as God is at work to reveal the idolatries that lurk in the hearts of church members, transforming them into the image of Christ, God is at work to reveal the idolatrous plans and dreams in the hearts of pastors, transforming them into loving shepherds of his people.

In his pre-Christian ministry mode, Paul was seeking to bring about God's purposes through coercive power, verbal and physical violence, and by transforming sinners into Torah-observant Jews in an effort to move God to save Israel. In Paul's mind, this would have taken the form of God unleashing resurrection on his people, driving the Romans from the land, vindicating the righteous, and restoring Israel at the head of the nations.

Paul was establishing a claim for participation in resurrection by elevating his social status and managing his image before others. He had assumed that the markers of his achieved status indicated something real about himself. They were his identity, the basis upon which he evaluated himself. He had presumed that his approval before others accurately reflected God's attitude toward him, and that on the day of judgment, Paul would be vindicated as one of the righteous among Israel for his rigorous Torah observance, his violent pursuit of sinners, and his commitment to the resurrection of Israel by Israel's God. All of this was about to change.

2

Conversion of Paul's Resurrection Imagination

In the previous chapter, I noted that Paul may have been among the groups of Pharisees who went out to hear Jesus in order to evaluate his messianic claims. In a discussion of the effects of Jesus's death and resurrection, Paul admits that he formerly had regarded Christ "from a human point of view" (2 Cor. 5:16), which is an admission that he previously viewed Jesus and his ministry through the lens of his inherited Pharisaic traditions. He shared the assumptions of his fellow Pharisees that Jesus was a dangerous figure who had to be destroyed (Mark 3:6). What did it mean that Paul saw Jesus "from a human point of view"?

Paul formerly conceived of Jesus as standing in the way of God's program of bringing about the salvation of Israel. The Pharisees were shunning sinners in order to avoid being contaminated by their inherent uncleanness and to shame them into repentance. While it is easy to assume that Pharisees simply avoided sinners and never gave them a second thought, they actually aimed to restore sinners and to foster in them the sort of Torah observance they approved. They thought that shutting sinners out was the way to make this happen.

Because of this, Jesus's behavior struck the Pharisees as reckless, irresponsible, and an offense to God. Rather than shunning and shaming sinners, Jesus was offering them hospitality, welcoming them to meals as honored guests, and taking up invitations to dine with them. Meals were intimate events, and eating together established social solidarity. Jesus was running the risk of developing a terrible reputation as one who did not care about Torah—God's word!—or about the salvation of Israel. Paul would have been among those who were offended by observing sinners listening to Jesus's teaching and his dining with them:

> Now all the tax collectors and sinners were coming near to listen to him. And the Pharisees and the scribes were grumbling and saying, "This fellow welcomes sinners and eats with them." (Luke 15:1–2)

Later, Luke records Jesus's encounter with Zacchaeus, a tax collector:

> He entered Jericho and was passing through it. A man was there named Zacchaeus; he was a chief tax collector and was rich. He was trying to see who Jesus was, but on account of the crowd he could not, because he was short in stature. So he ran ahead and climbed a sycamore tree to see him, because he was going to pass that way. When Jesus came to the place, he looked up and said to him, "Zacchaeus, hurry and come down; for I must stay at your house today." So he hurried down and was happy to welcome him. All who saw it began to grumble and said, "He has gone to be the guest of one who is a sinner." (Luke 19:1–7)

Tax collectors were regarded as traitors to the Jewish nation for collaborating with the Romans in extorting heavy fines and fees, becoming rich themselves and passing on money to the occupying power. Since God's salvation of Israel would have involved cleansing the land of the Romans and their traitorous agents, Zacchaeus was an ungodly stain who needed to be removed. He and the other tax collectors were among the "sinners" keeping resurrection realities at bay, reminders that the unclean Romans occupied God's holy land.

Not only was he a tax collector, but Zacchaeus was a leader among this group of traitors and had grown rich at the expense of his fellow Jews. This is why everyone who saw what Jesus had done was so upset at the fact that he had invited himself to dine as Zacchaeus's guest.

In light of Paul's aims, Jesus's behavior was an affront, both to God
and to national hopes for liberation from Rome. Sinners were not to
be treated as peers, as Jesus was doing, but to be shunned, rebuked,
and shamed. When Jesus earned the title "friend of sinners" (Matt.
11:19), it was not the sweet and tender title near to the heart of forgiven
saints. It was a dismissive epithet applied to one who was an obstacle
to the Pharisaic program of working to bring about resurrection.

Paul also would have sneered at Jesus's lack of credentials as a
teacher. There is no doubt that the Pharisees did their research on
anyone claiming to be a messianic figure. They were on the lookout for one who would come on the scene and raise hopes that the
great salvation they longed for was on the horizon. Perhaps Paul was
one who investigated Jesus's past, seeking to discover if he had an
impressive pedigree as a well-connected and honorable Israelite—
someone they could follow enthusiastically and behind whom they
could rally.

In a conversation with the Pharisees narrated in John's Gospel, the
issue of fathers arises. Jesus questioned whether they were truly sons
of Abraham since they were not acting like Abraham. The Pharisees
answered in a way that implies they had researched the circumstances
of Jesus's birth. "We are not illegitimate children," they said to him
(John 8:41). The implication here is that they know there were questions surrounding Jesus's birth. Perhaps there were rumors from his
hometown about the timing of his birth in relation to the marriage of
his parents that raised suspicions of misbehavior. After all, Mary had
conceived Jesus in her womb not long before she married Joseph. Jesus had a shameful past, which in Paul's view would have thrown grave
doubt on Jesus's messianic claims. How could someone conceived as
the result of sexual sin truly be the one through whom God would
bring about resurrection—salvation for his people?

Further disqualifying Jesus from fitting the messianic profile was
his posture of aloofness toward the Pharisees. He simply did not recognize their prestige, paying no respect to the social standing that
many of them had attained. In his conversation with Nicodemus, Jesus called on this "teacher of Israel" to disregard all of his accumulated

credentials and to begin all over again. When he exhorted Nicodemus to be "born again," he was urging him to receive the kingdom like a child—as one who had no social standing (John 3:1–10). And in his many confrontations with the Pharisees on other occasions, he regularly disregarded their acquired social status. This provoked animosity from them and drove them to jealousy when they saw that people were listening to him rather than to them.

Before Paul's conversion, when he evaluated Jesus "from a human point of view," Jesus was unimpressive, weak, and irresponsible. His fellowship with tax collectors and sinners made him unclean and appeared to be an effort to stand in the way of God's salvation. He had a shameful past and did not respect the social status of esteemed teachers. Because he regarded Jesus through the lenses of his inherited traditions, he saw Jesus as an affront to God, an obstacle to God's saving purposes. Paul would have agreed with his Pharisaic colleagues that Jesus was a threat, one to be eliminated. While he would have despised the Herodians—Jews who were collaborating with Rome in an effort to hold on to positions of influence and power—Paul would have agreed that it was the best course to plot with them to destroy Jesus (Mark 3:6).

Paul's Conversion on the Road to Damascus

After he heard of Jesus's death, Paul would have been certain that Jesus was not a messianic figure sent by God to effect resurrection realities for Israel. Not only had Jesus been killed by the Romans, but he was hung on a tree, clearly earning the verdict, "cursed by God" (Gal. 3:13; Deut. 21:23). When Paul discovered that a movement had sprung up claiming that Jesus had been raised from the dead and proclaiming him to be God's Messiah, Paul's mission was clear: he would lead an effort to stamp it out. These Jesus-followers were standing in the way of God saving his people for they were increasing the number of sinners in Israel. After cheering on Stephen's murder, Paul participated in a severe persecution of the followers of Jesus. He obtained letters from the Jerusalem authorities to go to Damascus to look for anyone

belonging to this movement and to bring them bound to Jerusalem.
Luke narrates what happened next:

> Now as he was going along and approaching Damascus, suddenly
> a light from heaven flashed around him. He fell to the ground and
> heard a voice saying to him, "Saul, Saul, why do you persecute
> me?" He asked, "Who are you, Lord?" The reply came, "I am Je-
> sus, whom you are persecuting. But get up and enter the city, and
> you will be told what you are to do." The men who were traveling
> with him stood speechless because they heard the voice but saw
> no one. Saul got up from the ground, and though his eyes were
> open, he could see nothing; so they led him by the hand and
> brought him into Damascus. For three days he was without sight,
> and neither ate nor drank. (Acts 9:3–9)

After this, Paul went into Damascus and his sight was restored by
a man named Ananias. There he learned that he had been appointed
to a completely different mission than the one he imagined—to proclaim Jesus as the Messiah to the gentiles. Given Paul's passion for
the resurrection of Israel, the clarity with which he understood how
this was going to work, and the conviction with which he pursued his
mission for the purity of the nation, it is difficult to imagine the stun-
ning reversal and the sudden clarity of Paul's new understanding. And
there is a wonderful gospel irony here: Paul had been vigorously striving to purify Israel from the contamination of foreign cultures and
he longed for the day when God would drive out the Romans so that
the land would be purified. Now, the God whom Paul was zealously
serving was sending Paul to preach God's salvation to those very nations and among those very cultures Paul had formerly despised.

We can speak of what happened to Paul as a "conversion," because
it is certainly a turning from one "way" to a radically different one.
But we can also speak of this as a divine arrest! The risen and exalted
Lord Jesus stopped Paul dead in his tracks and completely reversed
the course of his life. Paul had been fully convinced that Jesus had
made false claims to be Israel's Messiah and that his followers who

were proclaiming that God had raised him from the dead were now preventing God from saving Israel. He saw them as sinners, obstacles to God's resurrection program. In an instant, however, everything Paul knew was radically altered. God had not cursed Jesus but had raised him from the dead. This completely changed Paul's evaluation of Jesus, his followers, the nature of resurrection, and the character of the God of Israel. How could the God of Israel raise this cursed one from the dead? How could this companion of sinners be the first to take part in the resurrection? What does it say about the God of Israel that he has exalted the one with such a shameful past and who did not respect the prestige of the Pharisees? The powerful transformations taking place in Paul's imagination would have profound implications for the nature of Paul's ministry efforts to bring about resurrection realities on earth.

The God of Israel Vindicated Jesus

The moment Paul heard from the exalted Lord Jesus he knew exactly what had happened. The God of Israel had raised Jesus from the dead and exalted him to the heavenly throne. God had declared Jesus to be the "Son of God with power," indicating that his claims during his earthly ministry to be God's Son, the divinely appointed agent of salvation were entirely true (Rom. 1:4). God had vindicated Jesus, including his teachings and his way of life. When I say that God had *vindicated* him, I mean that in the face of previous opinions of Jesus such as Paul's—that he was an impostor, that he was cursed by God— *God fully endorsed Jesus's claims.* By raising him from the dead, God declared that Jesus is who he said he was, that he is the Son of God, the authoritative agent of salvation for Israel and the nations.

This encounter with the Lord Jesus led to a radical renovation of everything that Paul thought he knew. His understanding of Torah needed an overhaul in light of Jesus being the Christ. In addition, his ministry mode of coercive power in order to move God to act and bring about resurrection was exposed as tragically misguided. Thus far in his life Paul had been driven by power, force of personality, self-assertion, and verbal and physical violence. All of this was directed toward coercing sinners to repent and forcing God's hand to initiate resurrection. He now realized that his entire pursuit was a complete misrepresentation of the God of Israel. Rather than approving of Paul's pursuit and ministry mode, God had vindicated the life and the ministry mode of Jesus, who welcomed sinners and ate with them. God was pleased with Jesus who gladly accepted invitations to dine with traitorous tax collectors.

Paul had spent his life accumulating credentials and putting his best foot forward, striving to establish an identity of power, honor, and social status. He would have hidden any marks of shame from others, cultivating a personal presence of strength to avoid appearing weak or ineffective. He would have thought that his impressive resume and established identity as "righteous" would so impress God that he would have a prominent place at the resurrection. It is difficult to imagine the overpowering revolution in Paul's imagination when he realized that the God of Israel had vindicated Jesus who gave himself willingly to the shameful and disgraced death of a criminal on a Roman cross.

This moment on the road to Damascus revolutionized how Paul conceived of his pursuit of resurrection and vindication before God. The God of Israel does not vindicate the striver, the achiever, the honorable one, or the insider. He does not raise from the dead the one who meets all the culturally approved marks of identity, the one with all the credentials. God vindicates the one who calls for nonretaliation, for loving one's enemies—even the Romans; the one who gives himself up to shame, who comes in weakness and does not coerce. God raises the one who rejects violence and *becomes the object of violence*. This realization had a radical effect on Paul's outlook on everything. It truly brought about a conversion of Paul's imagination.

The Cross Is the Way to Resurrection and Exaltation

Paul reflects on the manner in which Jesus arrived at resurrection and exaltation in his letter to the Philippians. Overturning and reversing everything that Paul had formerly thought, Jesus forged the pathway to exaltation not through coercive power or pursuits of prestige, but through the humiliation and weakness of the cross. In exhorting the Philippians to embrace mutual service to one another in their community, Paul encouraged them to have the same mindset as that of Jesus Christ,

> who, existing in the form of God, did not regard equality with God as something to be exploited for his advantage, but rather expended himself, taking the form of a slave, becoming in human likeness; and being found in human form, he humbled himself, becoming obedient to the point of death—even death on a cross. (Phil. 2:6–8; my translation)

Paul notes that Jesus, before his incarnation as a human, existed in the form of God. He expresses this with a participial phrase (*hyparchōn*) that can be translated in several different ways: "*even though* he was in the form of God," or "*because* he was in the form of God." I will translate the expression, as some other major translations do, with the neutral rendering, "being in the form of God." Those that translate the expression in a concessive manner ("even though, although"), do so in order to highlight that Jesus expended and humbled himself *despite* the fact that he was God. But this indicates that Jesus acted in a manner that runs against the grain of his identity as God, as if this is something that God would not otherwise do. Others choose to translate the participle as *causal* ("because") in order to capture the reality that Jesus acted as he did precisely because of his identity as God.

Michael Gorman, in a wonderful discussion of how to regard this passage, advocates translating the expression as concessive ("although") in order to capture the radically counterintuitive manner in which Jesus acted. Jesus's behavior is counterintuitive because no other divine or human being does this. Anyone with such immense privileges exploits them to their advantage, seeking to gain even more. No one just gives up their privileges and prerogatives and takes extreme steps of self-sacrifice. This is the counterintuitive thrust that informs the "although." Once the interpreter reaches the end of the passage, however, and discovers that Jesus actually reveals God by what he does, Gorman envisions a return to v. 6 to reread the participle as causal ("because").[1] I think Gorman captures something crucial at the very heart of Paul here, and provides a strategic explication of how we encounter this text and have our thinking adjusted as we work our way through it. For our purposes, however, I will leave the translation "neutral" ("existing").

The important point here, at the start, is to note that Jesus existed in the form of God. And even though he did, possessing all conceivable advantages and privileges, he did not regard his existence as God as something to exploit for his own gain. As I indicated above, this is profoundly counterintuitive, since exploiting advantages is something that anyone and everyone else would have done. Certainly in the ancient imagination, dominated as it was by divine beings, this is how the gods behaved. This is also how we behave in the human realm. If we have an advantage, we use that to further our aims and goals, or to accumulate more possessions and further comforts. Jesus did something very different. *He expended himself,* pouring himself out, embarking on a downward trajectory that took him from the absolute cosmic heights to the lowest possible place. Becoming incarnate, he took the form of a slave and became obedient to God to the point of death—even to the point of a shameful death as a crucified criminal on a gritty Roman cross.

Gorman identifies the pattern of Jesus's life as "cruciform," a beautiful term that means "in the shape of the cross." Cruciformity has a "narrative pattern," identifying the movement of Jesus from having all privileges to his refusal to exploit them for gain to his self-expenditure and his willingly going to the point of death on a cross. This narrative pattern of cruciformity reoriented Paul's imagination of his life and ministry, as we will see in the following pages.

1. Michael J. Gorman, *Inhabiting the Cruciform God: Kenosis, Justification, and Theosis in Paul's Narrative Soteriology* (Grand Rapids: Eerdmans, 2009), 9–29.

Paul goes on to describe God's response to Jesus's cruciform pattern, his pursuit of a downward trajectory to the cross:

> Therefore God also highly exalted him and gave him the name that is above every name, so that at the name of Jesus every knee should bend, in heaven and on earth and under the earth, and every tongue should confess that Jesus Christ is Lord, to the glory of God the Father. (Phil. 2:9–11)

Paul's "therefore" in v. 9 indicates that God exalted Jesus *because of what Jesus did*. Because he refused to exploit his exalted status for his own gain, and because he utterly spent himself on behalf of others in faithfulness to God to the point of a humiliating and torturous death, God raised him from the dead and exalted him.

Jesus was not a messianic failure when he died on the cross, nor was it an indication of God's curse on him. Far from it! Paul discovered that the cross brought about Jesus's resurrection and exaltation. Not only this, but God gave to Jesus "the name that is above every name." The name God gives to Jesus is God's own name, "Yahweh," as is clear from the citation of Isaiah 45:23 in Philippians 2:10–11. In Isaiah 45:22–23, God declares:

> Turn to me and be saved,
>   all the ends of the earth!
>   For I am God, and there is no other.
> By myself I have sworn,
>   from my mouth has gone forth in righteousness
>   a word that shall not return:
> "To me every knee shall bow,
>   every tongue shall swear."

Paul identifies Jesus with the God of Israel to whom every knee will bow and every tongue confess as Lord.

God responded to Jesus's cross-directed course of life by labeling it with God's own name, indicating that the cruciform life of Jesus revealed God's own character. God vindicated Jesus precisely because Jesus faithfully and fully revealed the character of the God of Israel by pouring himself out unto death. This is why Gorman states that while we might translate the participle in Philippians 2:6 as "although" in order to capture the counterintuitive narrative pattern of Jesus, we end up regarding the participle as causal ("because") since what Jesus did is precisely what God does. It is in keeping with the character of God to forego privileges and pursue a course of self-expenditure.[2]

It is nearly impossible to imagine the power of this revolution that radiated through Paul's entire being. He previously would have been baffled or likely annoyed by Jesus's teachings. How on earth would loving enemies bring about resurrection? How would praying for the Romans ever do any good? How would welcoming sinners and eating with them ever get them to repent and be Torah-observant like the Pharisees? Indeed, Paul might have felt some satisfaction after hearing of Jesus's death. "Serves him right," he probably thought. "What an irresponsible teacher and a foolish and unrealistic way of life." God's vindication of Jesus changed everything for Paul. He realized that his use of force and coercive strength, his pursuit of prestige, and accumulation of credentials set him in an anti-God direction, one headed for destruction rather than resurrection.

Resurrection: Already but Not Yet

A further revolution dawned for Paul on the Damascus road regarding God's resurrection program. God had raised Jesus from the dead, but he was the only person to experience resurrection. This is not what the Pharisees—and almost all other Jews—were expecting. They thought that "resurrection" was to be one singular event when God would bring to an end the present age, raise the righteous dead, judge and destroy the wicked, and bring in the fullness of the new

2. Gorman, *Inhabiting the Cruciform God*, 29.

creation age—the kingdom of God. In one cosmos-wide act, the old age would be gone and the new age of Israel's liberation and creation's flourishing would begin.[3]

Jewish Expectation

The Day of the Lord
Resurrection of the Righteous/Judgment of the Wicked

But this is not what happened. Paul soon learned that at the cross, God dealt a death-blow to the present evil age and the powers that rule it. But its complete destruction awaited the future day of Christ. The cross also initiated the new age of resurrection life, but it would not come in fullness until that same future event. Paul, then, came to see that he lived at the crossover of the ages, with the new creation age of resurrection initiated by God in Jesus, and the enslaving grip of the evil powers over this world broken but not yet completely destroyed.

3. The idea of resurrection was well-established in Jewish culture in the first century, though its historical development is less than clear. It involved "the concrete act of God raising the dead from their tombs. Its theological dimensions include restoring and exalting God's covenant people, ushering in God's kingdom of justice and peace (or eternal life), and inaugurating God's new creation" (K. L. Anderson, "Resurrection," in *Dictionary of Jesus and the Gospels,* ed. Joel Green [Downers Grove, IL: IVP Academic, 2013], 775).

The Crossover of the Ages

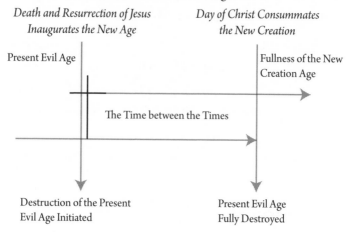

Death and Resurrection of Jesus   *Day of Christ Consummates*
Inaugurates the New Age   *the New Creation*

Present Evil Age

Fullness of the New
Creation Age

The Time between the Times

Destruction of the Present   Present Evil Age
Evil Age Initiated   Fully Destroyed

Discerning what this complex cosmic reality meant for God's people and how God wanted them to live in the world was no easy task. It occupied much of Paul's reflections, and his letters testify to the subtle wisdom needed to foster discernment among his church communities. We will have more to say about this in subsequent chapters, especially chapter four.

Resurrection Communities by the Spirit

When God exalted Jesus to his heavenly throne, God sent his Spirit into the world to form churches made up of local communities of Jesus-followers. Paul had formerly seen these communities as misguided sinners who were preventing God from initiating resurrection. He came to see, however, that these communities gathered as sites of resurrection presence. The resurrected Jesus is present among them by his Spirit, who radiates resurrection life within them and gathers them all up into resurrection power that redeems, renews, and restores. All those who participate in these communities of resurrection life will experience this reality in its fullness when Jesus returns and God unleashes resurrection life on all of creation.

The implications of these realities gradually dawned on Paul and are crucial for how we understand the church and ministry among the people of God. If resurrection has already happened and *is happening* among the followers of Jesus, then Paul was released from his pursuit of moving God to initiate resurrection and using coercive power on others. It cannot be manipulated or forced. Seeking to force God's hand to save is futile, since resurrection comes only by God's grace. Resurrection presence can only be enjoyed and inhabited by grace through cruciform postures of self-giving love, service, and celebration.[4]

Cruciform postures and habits of community life are what the church adopts now as it awaits the fullness of resurrection in the future. God poured out resurrection upon the singular person Jesus by his cruciform self-expenditure and love for others driven by obedience to the Father. This sort of joyful community life, therefore, sets the pattern for how the church awaits the future resurrection. Faithfulness to Jesus's mode of life means that we do not seek to coerce God nor do we coerce others to conform to expected behavioral standards in an effort to force God's hand. We celebrate what God has done in Jesus Christ by his Spirit, and we joyfully wait for God to act in the future, confident that he will do so.

Further, resurrection presence is encountered wherever people gather in the name of Jesus and adopt a cruciform identity. If God poured out resurrection life on Jesus because he willingly went to the cross, then cross-shaped communities are sites of resurrection presence. This was a powerfully countercultural message in the first-century Greco-Roman world that was oriented toward quests for honor and pursuits of power and prestige. It is no less countercultural in our day where a variety of pressures force churches to attract increasing numbers of people by appealing to cultural desires that are

4. Michael J. Gorman uses the expression "resurrectional cruciformity" to capture the paradoxical reality that resurrection life is cruciform and that cruciformity is the enjoyment of resurrection life (*Participating in Christ: Explorations in Paul's Theology and Spirituality* [Grand Rapids: Baker Academic, 2019], 53–76).

subtly shaped by the present evil age. We will have much more to say
about this in subsequent chapters.

God's resurrection presence in the church is a renewing power,
bringing healing to broken lives and restoration to fractured relationships. The redeeming presence of heaven is brought to earth in
cruciform communities, transforming our imaginations so that we
see the world as God sees it. It is not a world of limited goods where
we all must hoard and protect our stuff and pursue our own selfish
desires. The economy of heaven is among us, bringing new creation
life, abundance, and overwhelming us with blessing. Churches enjoy the superabundant realities of heaven by enacting cross-oriented
community behaviors that we find throughout the Gospels and Paul's
letters: confession of sin and forgiveness, service to one another, self-
giving love embodied through meeting one another's needs and offering hospitality to one another—especially to those on the margins
of our communities. Those experiencing loss, alienation, abuse, and
loneliness should find in churches a warm family welcome, loving
embrace, gracious hospitality, and respectful treatment.

Resurrection life can also be stirred up and enjoyed increasingly
by communities. The empowering and life-giving presence of God
by the Spirit has a multiplying effect! When a person in the church
repents of pride, crucifying their desires for honor and prestige, and
confesses that they have sinned against another person, and when
they are forgiven, resurrection life floods that relationship. Confession of sin and forgiveness require humility and weakness, so these are
cruciform behaviors, behaviors upon which God pours out life-giving
power. The presence and power of the age to come is radiated beyond the parties involved throughout the church so that the renewing
power of Christ by the Spirit is increasingly enjoyed by everyone.

When disciples take on cruciform postures by seeking to meet
needs, their hearts are overwhelmed with joy and delight and the
church is strengthened in faith to see that the future day of resurrection is indeed on the way. The tragic flipside is that when a community is dominated by postures and behaviors of selfish ambition,
pride, and anger at one another, the presence of this evil age is stirred

up. This radiates discouragement among the community and produces a loss of hope in God's power to transform.

Because of all of these realities, communities that want to experience resurrection power must be cruciform. That is the only way to enjoy the life of God among us by the Spirit. This conception of the church set in the midst of the present evil age—God's move to invade enemy territory by planting within it outposts of resurrection life—dawned on Paul as he reflected on his encounter with the exalted Jesus Christ on the Damascus Road. This vision reoriented Paul's conception of resurrection and it reshaped his life and ministry, as we will see beginning in the next chapter.

3

Conversion of Paul's Ministry Imagination

Paul's encounter with the exalted Lord Jesus on the Damascus Road thoroughly renovated his imagination, transformed his life, and overhauled his conception of God's resurrection program. He came to see that his ministry mode of power and coercion was tragically misguided, as was his personal pursuit of staking a claim for resurrection based on prestigious credentials and an approved social status. The realities of God's resurrection program dramatically upended his expectations. God raised the cruciform Jesus from the dead and had already begun creating communities of resurrection life that were shaped by the cross. These realities reshaped Paul's identity, his personal pursuit of resurrection, and the mode whereby he carried out his apostleship. In this chapter we will explore the facets of Paul's transformed imagination and in later chapters we will reflect on the specific practices this new approach entailed.

Reconfiguration of Identity as "Sinner"

Paul had previously regarded sinners as standing in the way of God saving Israel. Sinners among the people and traitorous tax collectors were preventing God from pouring out resurrection life. And Jesus was the ultimate sinner, for he was cursed by God when he was hung on a Roman cross, as Deuteronomy 21:23 says. After his encounter with the risen and exalted Jesus, however, Paul saw that his life pursuit to this point had not at all been in line with bringing about God's purposes. Far from it. He had, in fact, been fighting God, flying in the face of God's purposes.

Paul elaborates on this in Galatians 1–2. Rather than establishing an identity that would impress God and result in Paul's joyful participation in resurrection, he was actually attempting to destroy the church of God (Gal. 1:13). What he thought of as advancing God's cause was precisely the opposite. Paul saw that he was self-deceived. He had viewed the followers of Jesus as "sinners," a movement to be crushed through force. Now he saw himself as a sinner, one who was working directly against God's purposes.

Paul drew on this identity when he confronted Peter in Antioch. The church in that city was composed of Jewish and non-Jewish Christians, which must have supplied a complicated set of challenges to navigate. The social dynamics may have been challenging, but Barnabas—the main pastor—and other church leaders managed to foster a multi-ethnic community that shared meals together to demonstrate the reality that God in Christ had created them to be one new family by the Spirit. When Peter came from Jerusalem to visit the church in Antioch, he faced extreme discomfort because he was raised to believe that fellowshipping with gentiles was sinful. And even if he had already come to the conviction that God was including non-Jewish Christians in the one body of Christ, he had rarely rubbed shoulders with gentiles since the church in Jerusalem was made up of only Jewish Christians. When he came to Antioch, however, Peter fully leaned into the discomfort of eating with gentiles (Gal. 2:12).

At some point, however, some Jewish Christians arrived in Antioch from the Jerusalem church and Peter felt the pressure to remove himself from table fellowship with the gentile Christians (Gal. 2:12–13). Jewish Christians were still under the strong conviction that it was unlawful for them to go into a gentile's house or to have table fellowship with them—even gentiles who claimed to be Christian (cf. Acts 10:28). They assumed that gentiles were inherently sinful and that sharing a meal would be sinful and make them ceremonially unclean.

Paul knew all of this, of course, and after confronting Peter, he drew out the logic that was driving Peter's behavior. In Galatians 2:15, he acknowledges the common Jewish assumption that gentiles were sinners simply by virtue of their being non-Jewish: "We ourselves are Jews by birth and not Gentile sinners." He goes on to explain, however, that because God justifies a person without reference to ethnicity, even those whose identity is shaped by a Torah-based mode of life (i.e., Jews) must believe in Christ Jesus for justification. Paul knew that this was the crux of the issue for Jews like Peter and other Christians in Jerusalem. If they were justified on the same basis as non-Jews, then Jews were on equal footing with gentiles. They both stood shoulder to shoulder as they were justified on no other basis than faith in Christ. The reason they would have seen this as problematic is that sharing such a position with non-Jewish "sinners" would have made them unclean—they, too, would have been considered "sinners" because of their fellowship with gentiles.

Paul's strategy here is to draw out the Jewish Christian fear of fellowshipping with non-Jews and push it to its logical conclusion. In the end, Peter's action of removing himself from table fellowship with gentiles indicated that God's manner of justifying Jews and gentiles made Jesus a servant of the cosmic power of Sin. Does it really? "Certainly not!" is Paul's answer (v. 17).

Paul's argument in Galatians 2:15–21 is complicated but shows that Paul came to understand his status as an over-zealous member of a small party of those passionate for the purity of God's people was utterly irrelevant. Social status and ethnicity are not taken into account. Only one's relation to Jesus Christ matters. Because this put him on the same level as "Gentile sinners," Paul came to embrace his identity as "a sinner." This is no problem, since only "sinners" are justified by God.

On one hand, this is a *theological* reality for Paul, one with which we are familiar. Humans are sinners before God and stand in need of God restoring them to himself. Beyond that, however, this is also a *social* reality for Paul. That is, before his conversion, Paul, just like Peter, formerly looked down on gentiles as sinners. It was a term of exclusion, giving Paul the self-satisfied and superior sense that he was an approved insider. Labeling someone as an outsider empowered those who used this term of others to imagine that they were special objects of God's favor. "We're not like them, those ungodly sinners! Those people *deserve* God's wrath." Now, when he encounters such attitudes, Paul reminds his audiences of God's identity as the God who *justifies the ungodly* (Rom. 4:5). He also reminds his audiences of the kind of people who benefit from the death of Christ:

> For while we were still weak, at the right time Christ died for the ungodly. Indeed, rarely will anyone die for a righteous person— though perhaps for a good person someone might actually dare to die. But God proves his love for us in that *while we still were sinners* Christ died for us. (Rom. 5:6–8)

In addition, Paul does not see himself as a *former* sinner. He is *currently* a sinner. This is an identity he owns, stating emphatically: "The saying is sure and worthy of full acceptance, that Christ Jesus came into the world to save sinners—of whom I am the foremost" (1 Tim. 1:15). This is not to say that Paul is confused about his theological standing before God, as if he has forgotten that he is righteous and forgiven of his sins. And he is not celebrating an unrestrained pursuit of immorality. This is, rather, part of Paul's purposeful cruciform self-identity construction. Whereas he had formerly considered himself an insider with regard to his status with God, making so many others outsiders, he now happily owns the social status of sinner. The "establishment" that Paul belonged to considered Jesus a sinner and God vindicated Jesus and exalted him. Paul, therefore, gladly embraces the identity of sinner because it puts him closer to Jesus in his humiliation so that he can be with Jesus in his exaltation.

It is important to note that this is not a self-flagellating identity marker for Paul. He is not beating himself up or punishing himself for his former life. He happily owns this identity because it taps Paul into the power of the profound mystery of the death-resurrection dynamic that the cross creates. The mystery that Paul discovers—the secret

power of the wonder of cruciformity—is that because God poured
out resurrection life on Jesus when he went to the cross, God likewise
pours out resurrection wherever a person's life is shaped by the shame
and humiliation of the cross. To embrace the identity of being a sinner is a specific way that Paul can embrace shame and thereby have
his life and ministry flooded with resurrection power.

It may be very threatening or uncomfortable for pastors to self-
identify as sinners, but there is much promise in adopting an identity as an outsider with God as the only insider. This identity always
makes me the object of God's pursuit—I become one whom God is
always pursuing in passionate, redemptive love. I am not the arbiter
of who gets to have God dispensed to them. I am not the gatekeeper,
guarding the way to God. I stand alongside others whom God pur-
sues because of my inherent spiritual poverty. I am always in need,
and when I posture myself in this way toward God, I become the
grateful and joyful recipient of God's overwhelming faithfulness,
grace, and love. This posture is also inviting for others who feel beyond God's grasp or who are shamed by self-appointed members of
the "God Squad." It sets us alongside others, perhaps even sets us at
the head of the line of those whom God needs to sort out.

We may feel that such a posture is at odds with being a pastor, one
who is supposed to have God all figured out and should be ready with
a quick answer to any and every question. This sense, however, that so
much is riding on us drives ministry postures of arrogance rather than
of humility. Rather than seeing ourselves as "the authority" that must
have some sort of distance between the lay people and ourselves, we
can imagine the many ways that we can establish solidarity alongside
others. For starters, we can recognize that if we are in some sort of
pastoral ministry, then we are indeed the ones who study Scripture
in order to understand how we are objects of God's loving pursuit.
This does not, however, set us above or beyond anyone else. That is
simply our task, and we carry it out by explaining to others alongside
us how we can together enjoy God's love and kindness that are always
arriving into our fellowship by God's Spirit.

This is a very different posture from one in which I seek to distinguish myself from others, in some ways inhabiting a station above or beyond them. Many of us are used to imagining Christian development as a sort of spiritual progression where growth can be charted. Ministry leaders study the Bible and pray and therefore must be inherently closer to God—more "godly." They must be located on the chart far above and beyond the rest of us who merely exist in the daily mundane realities of life. This is not good for the church or for pastors.

Paul's burden was to establish himself socially alongside his sisters and brothers in the faith. In fact, he rhetorically situated himself at the front of the line of those in need of God's grace, rather than at some place above and beyond others. One way of embodying this is to develop relationships of mutual mentoring with people in the church that are located at the margins. A range of pressures arise from current ministry models that tempt pastors to cultivate and enjoy relationships with powerful or wealthy people in their churches. Notice this and resist it. Note who are the people in the church who for one reason or another are on the margins. They are not wealthy or powerful; they are not young and energetic or particularly attractive in some other way. These are people in our churches who do not often feel included and welcomed as valued members of God's one new family in Jesus.

These are also the people we can see as good gifts to us, for they can help us to remember who we are. If we keep in mind that Paul's identity as a sinner was both a theological and social reality, then we must realize that when we distance ourselves from those already marginalized, we are participating in a dynamic whereby we label them as "sinners" and regard ourselves as "righteous." This is self-deception, however, and we reveal that we are being entirely self-righteous and standing in need of repentance. We are denying about ourselves what Paul affirms about himself. But when we cultivate relationships with those that our church culture values less than others, we remind ourselves of our identities as people who matter no more or less than others. We also remind ourselves that we are part of a body of people who together are passionately pursued by God in Christ.

Further, we will find ourselves greatly blessed by the people among whom we minister. God longs to love and bless us through the entire body of people in our fellowship, not just a select few. Our worldly way of seeing things directs us to cultivate relationships only with those who are like us—those with whom we naturally feel comfortable. That feeling of comfort ends up cutting us off from the rich avenues of blessing we could enjoy if we were open to the entire body of Christ.

I have tried to take this seriously over the last several years as I participate in my church—embodying the theological reality of which Paul speaks through social practices. This is a challenge, I must confess, since I am a pretty serious introvert, and while I fully enjoy my friendships, I do not easily develop new ones and I do not enjoy small-talk, especially on a Sunday morning. I have tried, however, to be especially attuned to those on the margins of our community and initiate conversations with them, learning their names and hearing about their lives. And I am not doing this merely to make them feel welcome or to indicate that I am the source of spirituality and they are privileged to be speaking with me. I approach others in anticipation of being blessed by situating myself alongside a sister or brother in Christ, whether they are much older or younger, and hearing about their week, their triumphs and struggles, their joys and sorrows.

Ministry in Weakness and Shame Unleashes Resurrection

The counterintuitive way that God triumphed in Christ—by Jesus humbling himself and going to the lowest place, dying a shameful death on a Roman cross as a common criminal—determined Paul's mode of ministry. He embraced weakness and shame in his ministry, a radical departure from his former pursuit of prestige, exalted social status, and engagement in competition with fellow ministers. Paul had discovered this logic: since God raised Jesus from the dead and exalted him based on his faithful obedience unto a shameful death, God would flood Paul's life and ministry with resurrection power the more he lived and ministered from weakness and embraced the social shame that inevitably came his way.

Because Paul is the apostle of the crucified Lord, the measure of his faithfulness is when his life and ministry resemble as closely as possible a dying corpse on a Roman cross, for that is the site on earth on which God poured out resurrection life. Paul ministered from a posture of vulnerability and with a heart opened wide, and if that resulted in social shame, he embraced it. If he attempted to minister from some other posture or approach, he would not be drawing upon God's resurrection power. Some other source of power would be at work, one that was infinitely inferior, with no power to transform the cosmos, lives, and communities. For Paul, any other form or mode of ministry diminishes and marginalizes the power of the cross and forfeits any access to the transforming power of God.

In 1 Corinthians 2, Paul explains that when he originally visited Corinth he intentionally cultivated a personal presence and ministry mode that did not embody the "worldly wisdom" that he contrasts with God's wisdom in 1:18–31. When he refers to "worldly wisdom," Paul is referring to the way things are normally done in our culture. He has in mind our typical approaches that make sense according to social and cultural values we might find among those who know how to advance a cause, gain social prestige, or accumulate social capital. Worldly wisdom elevates strength and power, and exalts the rich, but God

> chose what is foolish in the world to shame the wise; God chose what is weak in the world to shame the strong; God chose what is low and despised in the world, things that are not, to reduce to nothing things that are, so that no one might boast in the presence of God. (1 Cor. 1:27–29)

The Corinthians loved powerful rhetorical displays and were drawn to a winsome presentation that was accompanied by well-spun oratory. Belonging to a social group with an impressive teacher or leader, according to corrupted Corinthian values, would elevate their social status, making their assembly an attractive one. Their leader's social prestige would rub off on all of them. But Paul did not play into these cultural expectations; rather, he intentionally flew in the face of them. He "did not come proclaiming the mystery of God to you in lofty words or wisdom. For I decided to know nothing among you except Jesus Christ, and him crucified" (2:1–2). He is referring not only to the content of what he preached, though he certainly has this in mind, but also to the way he carried himself.

He reveals the logic of his ministry mode in 1 Corinthians 2:3–5:

> And I came to you in weakness and in fear and in much trembling. My speech and my proclamation were not with plausible words of wisdom, but with a demonstration of the Spirit and of power, so that your faith might rest not on human wisdom but on the power of God.

Paul intentionally avoided carrying out his ministry among them with an impressive rhetorical display and a powerful personal presence. While it was counterintuitive to do so, had he persuaded them to follow the way of Jesus through such means, their faith would have been founded upon "human wisdom"—the logic of the present evil age—and not the power of God. To unleash the power of God among the Corinthians, Paul cultivated a personal presence of weakness. He was vulnerable and plainspoken. He did not try to impress them, but adopted a posture of invitation. Of course, doing so resulted in fear and trembling, since he thereby opened himself up to rejection and mistreatment. But he had to take these risks in order to draw upon God's power.

Something similar is going on in Paul's description of the founding of the churches in Galatia. Paul wrote a passionate letter to these churches after he heard that they were defecting from the gospel that he had originally preached to them. Jewish Christian teachers from Jerusalem had arrived and were convincing the gentile believers that they needed to convert to Judaism in order to experience the fullness of salvation in Christ. Paul saw this as a profound mistake and wrote the letter we know as Galatians to convince them not to take this step.

In Galatians 3:1–5, he refers to their original embrace of the faith, when they experienced the power of the Spirit (vv. 2, 5) and saw God work miracles among them (v. 5). He asks whether this all happened by their simply hearing with believing hearts, or by the "works of law" (vv. 2, 5). When he uses the expression "works of law," Paul has in mind the deeds based on Torah that indicate a Jewish identity. He is referring to the notion being considered among the Galatian churches that the true enjoyment of God's salvation in Christ only comes through a holistic conversion to a Jewish way of life (i.e, living a life characterized by a Torah-based identity). Paul obviously wants his audiences to see that this is not at all how God works among them. While God is saving Jewish people as Jews, he is also saving non-Jewish people (i.e., gentiles) as non-Jews, forming one new people out of all ethnicities in Christ.

Paul wants the Galatians to recall that God did not pour out saving power among them through conformity to Jewish ethnicity, but rather through a shameful public portrayal of Jesus Christ crucified (v. 1). "It was before your eyes that Jesus Christ was publicly exhibited as crucified!" What does he mean by this? Paul is referring to his original appearance in the area, which he recalls in Galatians 4:

> Friends, I beg you, become as I am, for I also have become as you are. You have done me no wrong. You know that it was because of a physical infirmity that I first announced the gospel to you; though my condition put you to the test, you did not scorn or despise me, but welcomed me as an angel of God, as Christ Jesus. What has become of the goodwill you felt? For I testify that, had it been possible, you would have torn out your eyes and given them to me. (Gal. 4:12–15)

When Paul was on his first mission with Barnabas, he was stoned to death in Lystra. Luke recounts this dramatic event in an understated way:

> But Jews came there from Antioch and Iconium and won over the crowds. Then they stoned Paul and dragged him out of the city,

supposing that he was dead. But when the disciples surrounded him, he got up and went into the city. The next day he went on with Barnabas to Derbe. (Acts 14:19–20)

This is probably the event that led to Paul's arriving in Derbe with the need to rest and recuperate from having been stoned. In Galatians 4:13, Paul refers to a "physical infirmity," which likely refers to his horrific physical condition after being pummeled with heavy rocks. After all, his physical condition "put you to the test"—that is, he looked so horrible that he would have made people physically react when they saw him. But the inhabitants of Derbe—one of the churches that received the Galatian letter—received Paul anyway, as if he were "an angel of God, as Christ Jesus" himself (v. 14). It was in this condition that Paul preached to them the gospel for the first time. In fact, Paul refers to this condition as a physical portrayal of Christ crucified. His brutalized and battered physical condition—being stoned to death, in Luke's telling—provided an opportunity for Paul to perform publicly the crucifixion of Jesus Christ. It was this condition that allowed Paul to take on the form of the cross and unleash resurrection power in his ministry.

Paul makes this dynamic explicit in 2 Corinthians 4, in a lovely poetic passage:

But we have this treasure in clay jars, so that it may be made clear that this extraordinary power belongs to God and does not come from us. We are afflicted in every way, but not crushed; perplexed, but not driven to despair; persecuted, but not forsaken; struck down, but not destroyed; always carrying in the body the death of Jesus, so that the life of Jesus may also be made visible in our bodies. For while we live, we are always being given up to death for Jesus's sake, so that the life of Jesus may be made visible in our mortal flesh. So death is at work in us, but life in you. (2 Cor. 4:7–12)

The death/life paradox revealed in the crucifixion and resurrection of Jesus Christ determined the nature of Paul's ministry vision whereby

ministry in weakness and shame unleashes God's power. The treasure of the gospel ministry is proclaimed by weak and unimpressive
ministers so that the power of the work of God in the world can be
plainly seen to be supplied by God and not from those who minister.
For Paul, the more impressive the minister, the less God's power is
at work. This reality, of course, means that God's faithful ministers
are regularly mistreated, beaten, crushed, and driven to despair. They
always carry themselves in ways that embody the death of Jesus so
that the resurrection life of Jesus can be revealed and unleashed in
them (v. 10).

For Paul, then, every conversation and every preaching opportunity must be imagined and anticipated in terms of how it might
be oriented by Jesus's death. How might he approach a person in
humility? How might he carry himself in terms of suppressing his
desire to be impressive? What social values are at work in every encounter that might run the risk of minimizing the cross? The dying
of Jesus shaped Paul's approach to ministry because that was the only
pattern of behavior that unleashed God's world-transforming power.
This death/life dynamic is at work in Paul's ministry to surround and
uphold Paul's own life and ministry with divine power.

The death/life dynamic is also at work in Paul's relationship with
his churches. He notes in v. 12 that death is at work in Paul and his
ministry team while "life" is at work among the Corinthians. That
is, the way that Paul ensures that God's resurrection life is working
among his churches is by giving himself up to death more and more.
So, when Paul shapes his daily life by the death of Christ, his own
life is flooded and sustained by God's resurrection power. And the
more Paul lives this way, the more his churches and those to whom
he ministers have God's resurrection life radiate into their lives.

The implications of this for contemporary ministry practice are
massive. If we want to see God work in power among our churches,
we will adopt approaches that embody the crucifixion of Jesus Christ.
How might this affect the ever-present temptation and tendency to ex-
ert control over others—other staff, lay ministry leaders, and various
ministries in a church? I was speaking with a friend recently whose
church experienced a thriving season characterized by joyful and

widespread participation. She reported, however, that recently there seemed to be a spirit of heaviness at the church. Lay ministers were pulling back from participating and discouragement was rampant. She indicated that the pastor seemed to have his hand in everything, offering advice that seemed more insistent than mere suggestion.

Ministry oriented by the cross provides space and clears room for others to jump in and participate. This approach trusts others and empowers them, since it is an approach taken by one always dying to self. Those oriented toward control and manipulation of others, however, will not see such an approach as promising. It will appear too risky. The outcomes cannot be predicted or controlled! And that is precisely the point. When our lives take the shape of the cross, we are completely given to God and to others and we do not control where we are going and how it will turn out. But we open up space for God to work in power, and the result of that dynamic is more promising and hopeful than church life that feels oppressive, stultifying, and suffocating.

Weakness, Shame, and the Display of God's Victory in Christ

We can also see this vision of Paul's ministry laid out when he discusses the nature of his apostleship in Ephesians 3. Many scholars rightly recognize that Ephesians 2 is the "heart" of this letter. In 1:15–19 Paul prays that his audience would gain insight into the mind-blowing resources God has given to the church in Christ, including the immeasurable power available for believers. Ephesians 1:20–2:22 is an extended elaboration of God's power, which Paul describes as the power exercised by God when he accomplished a victory in Christ's death and resurrection:

> God put this power to work in Christ when he raised him from the dead and seated him at his right hand in the heavenly places, far above all rule and authority and power and dominion, and above every name that is named, not only in this age but also in the age to come. And he has put all things under his feet and has

made him the head over all things for the church, which is his
body, the fullness of him who fills all in all. (Eph. 1:20–23)

Paul's claim that God has exalted Christ over all sorts of spiritual entities of cosmic authority in this age and future ages refers to hostile
cosmic powers arrayed against the rule of God. God's exaltation of
Christ indicates that in Christ's death and in God's raising him from
the dead, God won a victory over these figures who uphold, reinforce,
and rule over the present evil age.

How is this victory seen? Paul elaborates on this throughout
Ephesians 2. In vv. 1–10, God's triumph is seen as he rescues people
out of the enslaving death in which they were held by Satan, in alliance with other spiritual entities. God is transforming their lives, from
living in "death" through trespasses and sins (v. 1) to living in "good
works, which God prepared beforehand to be our way of life" (v. 10).
Paul further describes God's triumph in Christ in vv. 11–19. The hostile
cosmic powers of this present evil age had turned humanity against
itself through the cultivation of anger and resentment over ethnic, racial, and national distinctions (vv. 11–12). But in Christ, God is uniting
one new people made up of those from any and every nation, tribe,
race, and ethnicity. And when this one new people gathers, they do
so as God's new temple (vv. 20–22), which stands as a monument
to God's victory over the cosmic powers that have perverted God's
good world.

Based on this narration of God's victory in the death and resurrection of Jesus, Paul begins a second prayer report in Ephesians 3:1,
but he breaks it off in v. 2 to discuss the nature of his apostleship. Paul
feels the need to explain his circumstances—that he is praying for his
audiences as a prisoner. That is, if God is triumphant in Christ over
the hostile cosmic powers that have perverted God's good world, why
is Paul, his main representative, incarcerated? We need to keep in
mind that to be a prisoner in the ancient world would have raised as
many questions and had the same sense of social shame attached to it
that being a felon has in our day. If I met someone and in conversation
dropped the fact that I have been convicted of a felony, that might

make the other person end the conversation pretty quickly. Well, why is Paul in such a shameful and defeated situation if Jesus, the one he represents, is the Lord over all creation?

Paul explains this in vv. 2–13, helping his audiences understand that the manner in which faithful ministers embody God's triumph and depict the victory accomplished in Christ's death and resurrection is through weakness and joyful endurance of socially shameful situations. On one hand, Paul plays an exalted role in the work of God in the world. He was given a "commission of God's grace" for his churches (v. 2), which indicates that he is one of the handful of apostles charged by God to proclaim within creation the gospel of Jesus Christ. His role in God's saving program is crucial, for how else would the non-Jewish nations hear of the gospel unless he travels around proclaiming it?

On the other hand, Paul stresses his humiliation and weakened position. He is not doing this out of self-pity or from self-flagellation. He understands that the power of God is magnified if servants of Jesus Christ are in social positions of weakness and vulnerability. So he stresses that he is "the very least of all the saints" (v. 8), and adopts as a main feature of his identity that he is "a prisoner for Christ Jesus" (3:1; 4:1). This was a shameful social location for Paul to inhabit. According to the way that ancient people saw the world, for Paul to be in prison meant that the powers of the Roman Empire were more powerful than the God whom Paul served. And this is the striking contradiction that would have shaken up some of Paul's audiences.

But Paul notes that when he carries out his commission as a shamed prisoner in a weak and vulnerable social situation, and God forms the church through his preaching, God's glory is magnified throughout the cosmos (vv. 9–10). Paul depicts this in a striking passage. When he carries out his ministry and God builds his church— the one new temple (2:20–22)—this is the means whereby "the wisdom of God in its rich variety might now be made known to the rulers and authorities in the heavenly places" (Eph. 3:10). Just as in 1 Corinthians 2:1–13, God's wisdom here is his counterintuitive way of working. God chooses to accomplish his work in the world through people who are vulnerable and weak, and who accept the inevitable social shame that comes their way, even if that is being humiliated by being a felon for the cause of Christ.

According to the world's way of accomplishing things, God should choose someone with impressive credentials and lofty social status. An ideal candidate for "a commission from God" would be a Christian celebrity or someone with access to the halls of power. This is precisely the sort of culture in which many contemporary pastors and ministers carry out their work, and these are the strong currents and social pressures that shape their conceptions of ministry. They face the temptation to cultivate a persona of personal charisma and power, to carry themselves in such a way as to make strong personal impressions on others, and to project an air of competence that inspires confidence in people. For Paul, however, such ministry conceptions and their attendant postures and strategies are fraught with peril. They are precisely the sorts of ministry behaviors that diminish and drive away God's power. Because the powers and authorities have perverted the world with ideologies of power and quests for prestige, when ministries are built around powerful personalities they become organizations that diminish God's wisdom in the cosmic realm.

It is striking that Paul frames the "power in weakness" dynamic of his ministry in terms of God's conflict with the powers and authorities. As we will see in the next chapter, the cosmic dimensions of Paul's conception of ministry are critical to grasping a comprehensive understanding of cruciform ministry.

4

Pastoral Ministry in Cosmic Perspective

By this point we are starting to gain some perspective on the radical transformation of Paul's conception of ministry. But there is another dimension that we must grasp in order to fully understand his transformed approach. Along with most other Jews of his day, Paul envisioned all of reality in cosmic perspective. The human drama of daily life directly related to activity in the heavens, and all of reality was cosmically contested space. This had a massive effect on the transformation of Paul's mode of ministry, making it critically important for him to jettison his former ministry practices and to adopt new ones that were shaped by the cruciform pattern of Jesus Christ. For Paul, the world was held in the enslaving grip of evil cosmic powers, whose oppressive rule over creation was displayed in the orientation of human imaginations and behaviors toward sinful practices that kept them from enjoying the life of God. Prior to his conversion, Paul thought that his zealous efforts would play a key role in God's purposes for the cosmos—not only saving Israel but liberating creation from Satan and other hostile powers. He came to see at his conversion that his efforts were actually *furthering* the purposes of God's cosmic enemies. In this chapter, we will discuss how Paul saw the world, and how this larger cosmic context informed the transformation of Paul's ministry practices.

Drawing this larger cosmic perspective into our discussion of pastoral ministry is important because human attitudes, postures toward one another, and relational behaviors are directly related to spiritual realities that pervade and surround our communities. It is one thing to note that certain pastoral dynamics are unhealthy in certain ways, but this cosmic dimension makes things far more urgent than that. If we are operating in ministry from self-assertion or are seeking social power or prestige, we radiate into our communities the dynamics of the powers that rule the present evil age and seek the destruction of churches. On the other hand, when we embody the cruciform character of Christ, we stir up and radiate the life-giving and resurrection-powered presence of the Holy Spirit, resulting in renewal and dynamics of redemption. Human practices draw upon and are directly related to cosmic and spiritual realities. It is critical, therefore, that we understand the cosmic dimensions of earthly pastoral ministry.

The Present Evil Age

Paul's worldview, before and after his conversion, was "apocalyptic" in that he viewed reality from a cosmic perspective, involving a direct relationship between activity in the heavens and life on earth. God had originally intended for humanity to rule over creation on God's behalf and for God's glory. As humanity flourished and oversaw the spread of fruitfulness through all of creation, they manifested and enjoyed the reign of the creator God who filled creation with God's glory. This is the way that God had intended for the earthly realm and the heavenly realm to relate to one another—earthly realities reflected heavenly realities. Because of humanity's rebellion, however, that scenario has been ruined. But the problem is much greater than human sinfulness. In the complex character of the present evil age, the sinfulness of humanity points to a larger cosmic reality.

Jews of Paul's time knew very well that they were living in an era in which God's will was not being done on earth. The present age was filled with oppression, suffering, and the apparent triumph of evil. Epitomizing the evil character of the current time period was the reality that Israel was not flourishing under the reign of Israel's God as God had intended. Jews believed that this age was one of pain and suffering, in which the righteous also suffered, but that God would call a halt to this age at some point and bring in the new creation age. This would be an age of life from the dead, a time of restoration for Israel, of relief from suffering when all of creation was renewed and Israel finally experienced the reign of the one true creator God who was the God of Israel.

Paul makes several references to this present evil age throughout his letters. He remarks that Jesus Christ "gave himself for our sins to set us free from the present evil age" (Gal. 1:4). In Colossians 1:13, he refers to this age as a realm that is spatial and temporal, calling it "the power of darkness." In Ephesians 2:2, he refers to "the age of this world" (*ton aiōna tou kosmou toutou*), and later writes that "the days are evil" (Eph. 5:16). In the midst of a well-known passage on divine warfare, he refers in Ephesians 6:12 to cosmic figures that oversee "this present darkness" (*tou skotous toutou*).

All of this is to say that Paul shared the worldview of many of his fellow Jews who believed they were inhabiting God's created world during a time period when it was dominated by evil. Paul's hope before his conversion was that his efforts to bring about a righteous and law-observant Jewish people would result in God's transformation of creation—his bringing about the destruction of the present evil age and the initiation of the new creation. That future age would be the era of salvation, the time when God would bring about all the hoped-for resurrection realities for Israel—the righteous would be vindicated by God and Israel would be free of their enemy oppressors. All of God's people would experience the overwhelming blessings of the land's flourishing and productivity, and all of creation would be renewed.

The Rulers of This Age

The present age, according to Paul, is not just a period of time in history, nor is it a static reality. It is overseen and ruled by hostile cosmic powers that provide the "present evil age" with a logic and rationality—an operating dynamic. It is an all-encompassing matrix of oppression that involves the heavens and the earth, down to the very fabric of creation, and affects cultural imaginations, human relationships, and communities. A range of cosmic powers conspired together to see to it that this enslaving reality prevented humanity from experiencing God's good world as one of flourishing as God had intended. It is critical for us to understand our cosmic enemies and just how they do their work, since they have such a massive effect on human relationships, including ministry practices.

Satan

One of these actors is Satan, God's main cosmic enemy, a spiritual figure opposed to God's purposes. Paul calls him "the god of this age" (2 Cor. 4:4), indicating that the world during this time period lies in his grip and under his reign. He also calls him the "ruler of the power of the air," overseeing a spirit that works among sinful humanity (Eph. 2:2). "The air" is the realm of mindsets, ideologies, cultural assumptions and prejudices, hopes, fears, animosities, and even national and tribal commitments. Satan, then, works at a very broad level, ensuring that cultural fears and suspicions of others are stirred up so that various groups demonize and mistreat one another. He sows ideologies, mindsets, and sinful patterns within the world that look attractive but that ultimately lead to degradation and self-destruction.

In 2 Corinthians 11:14, Paul says that Satan presents himself as "an angel of light"—as a figure whose ways appear winsome, attractive, and promising. The ideologies and ways of life that he sows within the world are tempting to humanity because they seem hopeful, practical, and make good sense—they are how things get done! He draws people into modes of life oriented by respectability and cultural approval. He tempts humanity to pursue apparently good ends through power, pursuits of prestige, and prominence. While on the surface, such ways of life do not appear to be greedy, selfish or self-seeking, the dynamics at work at the motivational level and the deeply embedded behavioral patterns are oriented away from the cross in such subtle ways that it is almost impossible to notice.

The Powers and Authorities

Along with Satan, Paul refers often to other cosmic figures who have authority over this age—the powers and authorities (Gal. 4:3, 9; Eph. 1:21; 3:10; 6:12; Col. 2:8, 20; Rom. 8:38–39; 1 Cor. 2:6, 8). Called by various names, these figures are in some mysterious way allied with Satan. They are cosmic figures to whom God had granted authority over creation and who have in some way rebelled. According to the Jewish worldview that shaped Paul's thought, these figures were called the "sons of God" in Genesis 6:1–4 and were given positions of cosmic authority by God, commissioned to orient the lives of nations so that their cultural patterns were characterized by justice (Deut. 32:8; Ps. 82:1–8). They rebelled, however, by breaking through the barrier separating the physical and spiritual realm; they took on bodies and had sexual relations with women. Because of this, a significant number of them were kept in some sort of cosmic prison to await their judgment at the great day of the Lord (2 Pet. 2:4; Jude 6).

We get a glimpse of these figures in action in Daniel 9–10. After Daniel prayed a great prayer of confession for the sins of Israel (Dan. 9:1–19), he was visited by the archangel Gabriel who had been dispatched by God to visit him. He informs Daniel that it had taken him three weeks to arrive because he had been opposed by "the prince of the kingdom of Persia," though the archangel Michael had come to his aid (10:13). After delivering his message, Gabriel told Daniel that he was going to depart and would face the princes of Persia and Greece (v. 20). This is quite a remarkable window into the cosmic drama that shapes the biblical and Jewish view of the world. Archangelic rulers orient the lives of nations, sowing cultural patterns and society-wide mindsets to ensure that humanity is idolatrous and does not experience life in God's world according to God's design.

These are the figures that Paul calls the powers and authorities, who, along with Satan, uphold and oversee this present evil age, having sown within the various cultures of the world patterns of life that are enslaving and oppressive. That is, they are designed to hold people in spiritual death (Eph. 2:1). Patterns of life such as greed, living for the fulfillment of sexual pleasure, and being governed by unrestrained sensual desires keep people trapped in death, headed for eternal destruction. They are the figures behind ideologies that encourage people to pursue the fulfillment of personal ambition without regard to how much they harm other people, including themselves. These ways of life and a countless variety of others are made available within this age for humans to walk in. For Paul, sinful patterns of life and unjust social systems are not merely evidence of human disobedience. They come from somewhere; there is a logic behind this complex network that makes up our perceived reality. This is all a manifestation of the work of the powers and authorities, the rulers of the present evil age.

Sin, Death, and Flesh

Making the situation even worse is the presence of several other cosmic invaders that have hijacked God's good world—Sin, Death, and Flesh. Paul envisions these cosmic entities as active, having their own minds and wills. In Romans 5, Paul speaks of Sin and Death as coming into the world (v. 12), and Death as spreading and exercising dominion (vv. 12, 14). He also depicts the insidious genius of Sin in Romans 7. God's "law is holy, and the commandment is holy and just and good" (v. 12), but Sin, "seizing an opportunity in the commandment, produced in me all kinds of covetousness" (v. 8). Sin came alive, "deceived me and through [the commandment] killed me" (v. 11). Sin and Death, for Paul, are active agents, along with Flesh, cosmic actors that turn God's law into an unwitting accomplice of cosmic enslavement.[1] They have a genius for turning God's good gifts into opportunities for oppression and human enslavement.

---

1. Tremper Longman III and Daniel G. Reid, *God Is a Warrior* (Grand Rapids: Zondervan, 1995), 161.

Many of us are familiar with Paul's language of sin, death, and flesh, though we imagine these as realities that each individual human experiences. That is, we all sin and will all die at some point, and we are all made of flesh. While this is true, as far as it goes, in Paul's apocalyptic worldview, these are also cosmic entities that conspire together to corrupt God's good purposes. They distort the best of human intentions, as Romans 7 reveals, hijacking even the good motivations of well-intentioned people who want to obey God's word revealed in Scripture. As Paul says in Galatians 5:17, Flesh wages war against God's Spirit so that humanity's best intentions are constantly frustrated. When humanity sinned against God, these cosmic forces mysteriously entered the stage of the human story and began working to further oppress humanity, twisting and distorting human experience so that we desire what will do us harm. These entities also corrupt community dynamics in subtle—and some not-so-subtle—ways so that people do harm to one another and ultimately destroy one another. They turn even our best aims and plans toward destruction so that, as Paul discovered, they end up furthering our experience of cosmic enslavement.

Some interpreters have called this collection of cosmic figures— Satan, the powers, and Sin, Death, and Flesh—the "apocalyptic power alliance," referring to the entities that conspire to ensure that human experience in this world is enslaving, and people are trapped in spiritual death.[2] God had created this world to be an arena for the flourishing of humanity as we ruled creation for its constant renewal and our own enjoyment—all for God's glory. While modern Christians are well aware of the story of human sinfulness and rebellion against God's purposes, we are less acquainted—or perhaps not at all—with Paul's view of our cosmically enslaved world. Having hijacked God's good world, these cosmic entities exploit human sinfulness, dominating humanity and holding all of creation in their enslaving grip. The situation is far more hopeless than we may have previously realized!

2. J. Christiaan Beker, *Paul the Apostle: The Triumph of God in Life and Thought* (Philadelphia: Fortress Press, 1980), 190.

Cosmic Enslavement: Practices, Patterns, and Postures

So, how does this cosmic scenario relate to how Paul conceives of his churches' community life, and ultimately, to pastoral ministry? For Paul, the enslavement of the cosmos to the apocalyptic power alliance shows up in human experience through practices, community patterns of behavior, and postures that people adopt toward each other that are all characterized by mistreatment of one another, exploitation, oppression, a singular pursuit of satisfying sensual desires, and the pervasive discontentment that fuels greed, selfish ambition, and quests for power.

Throughout much of 1 Corinthians, Paul warns the church against community dynamics of division and postures of arrogance on the part of the rich toward the poorer members of the church. Paul discerns that these splits, factions, and animosities flow from their living according to the corruptions sown within the cosmos by hostile cosmic powers. Paul claims they are drawing upon the "wisdom of this age" in their community dynamics, because their corporate imagination is shaped by triumphalism, conquest, domination, and power-seeking. These postures toward others and the corrosive community dynamics they inevitably generate represent on earth the enslavement of this world to "the rulers of this age" (1 Cor. 2:6). Paul goes on to say that "[n]one of the rulers of this age understood" God's wisdom, "for if they had, they would not have crucified the Lord of glory" (v. 8). The way God works is counterintuitive to the logic that drives the hostile cosmic powers, which is all about power, prestige, pleasure-fulfillment, domination of others, agitation for control, exploitation of the weak, and self-advancement at all costs.

Cosmic enslavement shows up in the human realm wherever there are practices and community patterns of destructive competition, such as (1) divisive community dynamics where a few competing community leaders gather to themselves people who are loyal to them rather than ultimately to Christ; (2) divisions along racial, ethnic, and socio-economic lines; (3) outbursts of anger, denunciation, and condemnation; and (4) when some community members are made to feel they are second-class citizens, or in some way unwelcome. We may detect the work of God's cosmic enemies whenever and wherever we witness God's order of flourishing being ruined in some way.

This is the crucial point to grasp: These practices, patterns of community life, and postures toward others are all sown within the world to make manifest that hostile cosmic forces hold God's good world in their enslaving grip. These behaviors all flow from the rulers of the present evil age and when humans live in these ways, we reinforce their enslaving grip over creation. And this is the great irony: before his conversion, Paul thought he was fighting the powers of the present evil age on God's behalf. But in his zealous ministry mode, he was actually serving the purposes of the apocalyptic power alliance to ensure that humanity did not enjoy God's gracious reign. His coercion of sinners, his pursuit of power, his quest for prestige, his accumulation of credentials, and his competitiveness with his ministry colleagues—all of that was not only misguided, but it was the manifestation of his enslavement to the present evil age and its anti-God powers. Paul came to see that all of his efforts were positively working to further Satan's reign as "god of this world" (2 Cor. 4:4). This scenario not only fueled the transformation of his ministry, it had a massive effect on how Paul thought theologically and diagnosed problems in his churches.

Contemporary ministry is filled with temptations to adopt attitudes, postures, and behaviors that draw upon and reinforce cosmic enslavement. A pastor may grow discontented with her church, either by its small size, its lack of growth or by its failure to live up to her expectations. Perhaps she has heard about a colleague enjoying a blessed season where his ministry is flourishing in another city and wonders why she is not experiencing the same sorts of dynamics. She wants the best for her church and may be tempted to examine her congregation for its weaknesses and failings, adopting an attitude of judgment toward those she views as holding the church back. She may cast about for strategies to motivate her lay leaders to improve themselves and redouble their efforts in order to produce the sort of excitement and energy she sees in her colleague's church. I have witnessed this very dynamic take place in several churches, inevitably propelling pastors to adopt motivational strategies oriented by manipulation and coercion that generate dynamics of the present evil age—discouragement, division, and destruction.

I knew a pastor in a small town who traveled to a church growth conference at a massive church in a major city and grew enamored with its strategy for growth. He returned with armfuls of binders and notebooks for his lay leaders to study in order to implement the plan about which he was excited. But over the subsequent years his constant desire to "take the church to the next level" made him apply pressure to his team of volunteers that ended up burning them out and leaving him frustrated. In his mind, he was motivated by a desire to reach people with the gospel, and to get people excited about the life of the church. His coercive manner, however, stymied his efforts. Rather than producing the good outcomes he envisioned, he ended up transforming the church ethos from one of joyful rest and refreshment into one characterized by pressure and high expectations. Leaders felt that they were always being evaluated and judged. The pastor no longer saw the people in his church as gifts from God to be cared for, nurtured, and enjoyed. He now viewed them critically, examining them in terms of whether they were the sort of people who could attract even more attendees and "giving units." He ended up leaving town to take another church on another continent, and left the community wondering what was next.

I have seen the dynamics of good intentions manipulated toward destructive ends in churches filled with young families. An earnest young couple may discover a well-packaged parenting strategy that comes ready-made with books, videos, and workbooks, promising to point the way to fostering family life that honors God. They form a class focused on working through the curriculum, discussing how to prioritize their marriage and how to relate to and discipline their children. How could such an effort to form healthy, God-glorifying families be a bad thing? Over time, however, the almost imperceptible dynamics of corruption begin to manifest themselves as participants in the class subtly pass judgment on families who do not relate to their children according to the approved strategies. Participating families begin to assess who is truly cultivating family life in ways that "honor God." Parents with children who present behavioral challenges feel shamed and guilty that things are not working out as they had hoped. Before long, stresses and factions begin to develop in the church much like we find in Corinth. I have known more than a few pastors who have had to deal with the fallout of situations like this.

In each of these instances, and in many more I could mention, apparently good intentions are manipulated by the powers of the present evil age to produce the destructive fruit of community division and discouragement. This is because the imaginations of pastors and church members are naturally oriented by the "wisdom of this world." If we are not discerning and critically self-reflective about our mindsets and our conception of the life of the church, our hearts will inevitably grow discontented. We will see how we can improve on the character of our churches by enacting various strategies without realizing that we very well may be drawing upon the dynamics of the present evil age. We may have good aims, but our approach may be dominated by coercion, judgment of others, and manipulation so that the good we intend to do will be distorted by destructive powers. Paul's "I" in Romans 7 delighted in the law of God, but he did not take full account of the genius of Sin, always lurking to seize upon good motivations and turn them against God's people to produce the fruit of Death.

The Death of Christ and New Creation Space

Paul came to see that the enslaving grip of the present evil age would not be broken by any human effort, not even by passionately faithful Pharisees producing a nation of fellow Jews who diligently observed Torah. The plight of the entire cosmos was much darker and more all-encompassing than anything humanity could do to solve it. God himself broke the hold of the apocalyptic power alliance over creation in order to liberate humanity to experience the life of God on earth for God's glory. God came in Christ, who, as a human, became a full participant in the cosmically enslaved situation (Rom. 8:3; Gal. 4:4–5), and whose death dealt a cosmically powerful mortal blow to the powers that had seized God's good world. His death broke loose their enslaving grip, and it served notice to them that their reign would come to an end at the final day of judgment (1 Cor. 2:6). While the cross dealt a decisive blow to these anti-God forces, God's final victory over them will come when he destroys them for good at the day of Christ (1 Cor. 15:24–26).

This is the cosmically contested situation in which Paul envisions the church. The church in the world is the sign of God's victory over the apocalyptic power alliance—Satan, the powers and authorities, and Sin, Death and Flesh. God has *already* struck a fatal blow to his cosmic enemies and has shaken loose the grip of the present evil age over creation, but he has *not yet* accomplished his final victory. This world remains, therefore, enemy territory, still held in the grip of the god of this age and the evil powers. But God has invaded enemy territory and has begun establishing and growing communities of Jesus-followers—the worldwide church. God's Spirit fills and pervades these communities, giving them life and animating them. God dwells within them by his Spirit, filling the space with resurrection life. These communities, then, are locations of resurrection life and power, spaces that are liberated from the dominating influence of the powers and that bring renewal, redemption, restoration, and life.

According to the mystery of Paul's gospel, God has chosen to liberate the cosmos over time rather than all at once. God will fully flood all of creation with his presence by the Spirit, pervading all things with resurrection life. God will thoroughly renovate the cosmos, cleansing it of all the destructive influences of those malignant cosmic forces. We look forward to this day with great hope and anticipation. Before that day, however, God is filling the church with resurrection life, which is God's own life-giving power. The sort of existence that will characterize the new creation when it comes in its fullness—bringing life, satisfying hearts, renewing relationships, and healing injuries and wounds—that mode of existence is present now in churches by the Holy Spirit. Churches are outposts of the kingdom of God in enemy territory, locations of resurrection life in the midst of death, arenas of new creation set within the present evil age.

Paul came to see that it was the death of Christ that brought about this reality. And this is the point I have been driving at in drawing our attention to the church's cosmic situation: Paul discovered that churches can only enjoy God's resurrection presence when they adopt cruciform patterns of life.

The Cross Is the Operating Dynamic of New Creation Space

Because the cross is the means whereby God shattered the enslaving grip of the present evil age and created the church, the cross determines the behavioral patterns and relational practices of new creation communities. God's victory was brought about in Christ when he poured himself out and faithfully obeyed to the point of a shameful death on a Roman cross. His cruciform life now pervades the communities that gather in his name and that are filled by the Spirit of Jesus (Phil. 1:19). God is shaping these communities into the image of Jesus Christ, growing and nurturing them into what Jesus Christ would look like on earth if his cruciform life took community form (2 Cor. 3:18).

This is not merely an interesting bit of New Testament biblical theology. It is critically important for understanding the cosmic significance of behavior in the church and of ministry practices, postures, and modes of relating.

We can see this in 1 Corinthians 1:18–2:16. Paul discusses the logic of the cross that animates the church, and how it runs directly counter to the logic of the enslaving present evil age overseen and oriented by hostile cosmic powers (1:20). He refers at several points to "the wisdom of the world" throughout this passage. When Paul uses the term "wisdom," he is referring to an operating dynamic—a set of assumptions and a collection of mindsets, behaviors, and relational postures—a total way of community life. There is, then, a "wisdom of this world," or, the present evil age, and there is a "wisdom of the cross." I use the term *logic* to capture how these competing wisdoms include ways of thinking and modes of relating. The logic of the world is oriented by pursuits of power, prestige, accumulation of wealth, and the exaltation of some people over others. "Worldly" ways of doing things involve putting on impressive displays and motivating people to join a movement based on the promise of being associated with a powerful and impressive figure.

But this is not the logic upon which God is building the church. It simply does not represent God's way of working, but the very opposite. God is most clearly revealed in the cruciform Jesus (Phil. 2:9–11), and he triumphs over the powerful anti-God cosmic rulers in the death of Christ (Eph. 1:20–21; 2:13–16). According to a worldly logic, this makes absolutely no sense at all. God's ways are completely counterintuitive to the ways of the world. Whereas the world envisions victory by winning, God triumphs by losing. He conquers the powers of evil by dying. That is utterly backward and ineffective according to the logic of the world—it is *foolishness* (1 Cor. 1:23). The cross, however, is the most strategic depiction of how God operates. It represents his very character, it indicates how he achieves victory, and it determines the mode of life for God's people who embody God's presence as the church.

It is always tempting for the church to accomplish what we perceive as God's ends through worldly means. This is the perpetual stumbling block of God's people. Our imaginations are revealed as worldly and thoroughly shaped by the present evil age when we envision possibilities for accomplishing godly goals through developing relationships with powerful and influential people, raising vast sums of money, or rallying behind a compelling Christian celebrity. The church throughout the ages has constantly fallen prey to the temptation to cultivate relationships with political power in hopes of somehow accomplishing God's purposes. These are all strategies that come directly from the present evil age and can only produce its fruit. They are sourced in quests for power, selfish ambition, and greed—all things Paul warns about.

Cruciform Ministry and the Powers

Paul's cosmic conception of the church as an entity created and nurtured by God's Spirit within the hostile cosmic territory of the present evil age has loads of relevance for Paul's transformed mode of ministry. His ultimate aim before his conversion had been to produce on earth the resurrection realities associated with God's salvation. He longed for the liberation of Israel from Roman oppression, and hoped and prayed for the new creation realities of resurrection life to be poured out on earth. This vision drove his zeal for the purity of Israel. He had come to see, however, that his ministry mode of coercion and violence, along with his exclusion and forceful condemnation of sinners, were furthering the enslaving grip of the apocalyptic power alliance. Far from zealously serving the God of Israel, he was fostering the oppressive hold of the present evil age over creation. His quests for power and personal prestige, his cultivation of image and pursuit of an elevated social status, and his competitive spirit were stirring up and radiating the destructive dynamics of the present evil age.

Eventually, Paul discerned that faithful ministers of a cruciform Lord pursue new creation ministry goals with new creation means. He had formerly been trying to accomplish new creation goals with means drawn from the present evil age. This is self-destructive and self-defeating. His conceptual revolution is reflected in his question put to the Roman Christians: "Should we continue in sin in order that grace may abound?" (Rom. 6:1). While the answer is obvious, Paul realized he formerly had fallen prey to this very strategy. But only new creation means can produce new creation fruit. Only cruciform behaviors, postures toward others, speech patterns, and relational dynamics can bear resurrection fruit in community life. God only pours out resurrection life on Jesus's cross and on modes of life shaped by it. It can be no other way.

For Paul, cruciform ministry practices are the only way to foster new creation life among God's people. Ministry modes, postures, attitudes, and practices that embody the weakness and "foolishness" of the cross stir up and radiate resurrection power among God's people. This dynamic results in renewal, with relationships being restored and lives being transformed. Discerning pastors constantly resist ministry modes that draw upon and embody the logic of this world, since these stir up and radiate the enslaving and oppressive dynamics of the present evil age. This reality that takes into account cosmic dynamics is why the passionate efforts of so many pastors fail to produce the new creation fruit they envision. It is why pastors who see themselves as motivated by commitment to God often apply pressure to people, rather than offering them relief and rest, driving people away or provoking resistance from their churches. They may tell themselves that there is something wrong with their congregants, but it is worth considering whether their ministry efforts are stirring up and radiating dynamics of the present evil age. As Paul wrote in Romans 7, while they may be delighting in the law of God in their minds and intentions, they end up discovering a different dynamic at work in the body of Christ. How can it be that my good intentions have produced the dynamics of death? Perhaps unintentionally, such ministry efforts may be manipulative and subtly coercive so that the results are community dynamics of division and discouragement.

Cruciform Practices of Conflict Resolution

This cosmic perspective has the potential of bearing great fruit in pastoral ministry. It is an approach that recognizes our postures toward others, our attitudes, and our behaviors have the potential to stir up and radiate within relationships either the dynamics of destruction or the power of the resurrection. It has changed the way I envision conflict. Formerly, when I had to confront a situation, I was driven by my fears and took an approach oriented toward power and control. I had seen the other person as in the wrong and I was going to vindicate myself as in the right. I prepared to argue my case and back a person into a corner, demonstrating where he had gone wrong and how he needed to repent and get back on the path of righteousness.

I took such an approach with a ministry partner with whom I had a sharp disagreement. We arranged a time to get together, and in advance of that meeting I prepared all of my arguments. I anticipated the moves he might make to fight off my arguments and armed myself with counterarguments. I recalled other situations in which he had done something similar and was ready to call to mind previous failures in order to demonstrate to him that he had a pattern of causing trouble. In the time before our meeting, I grew angry and was nearly ready to explode.

When we met, I was ready for a fight. I envisioned him as a problem that I needed to solve. I was not even listening to him as he initiated our conversation, looking for an opening to rehearse all my finely-honed arguments. Convinced of the righteousness of my cause, I began laying out my case. Reacting as anyone would who was being cornered and judged, he became angry and began hurling accusations at me, to which I responded by bringing up some hurtful things from his past.

I am glad to say that after a while, we both came to our senses and realized we were at an impasse. Without resolving anything, we agreed to meet again soon to sort things out. Reflecting later on our conversation and on the manner in which I approached him, I realized that I had employed a strategy that was guaranteed to generate destruction. I had assumed the worst about him—that he would not be interested in doing me good, but only intended my harm. I had approached him from a posture of fear, which created in me a desire to get the upper hand in our discussion, to come to him with power and force him to see things my way. In an effort to set things right, as I envisioned the situation, I put him on the defensive and provoked him to respond to me sinfully, which he did. I had stirred up and was radiating the presence of the powers of this evil age since I had approached the situation from a posture and with language supplied by the cosmic figures that work to destroy community life.

I approached our subsequent interaction very differently. Knowing that God only floods relationships with resurrection life where people adopt cruciform postures, I thought about how the cross might orient a different strategy. Rather than seeking to gain leverage in our relationship, I decided to give all my leverage away at the start of our conversation. I reoriented my conception of him, no longer seeing him as an opponent, but as my friend who longed to do me good. I put myself in his hands and began our conversation by confessing my sin. I told him that I had sinned against him by assuming the worst of him and that I previously came to him with a desire to triumph over him rather than to reconcile with him. I asked him to help me understand how he saw things and how he understood the conflict between us. As he spoke, I listened intently. I wanted to honor him and give him the gift of being truly heard.

In the end, we both felt that we had listened to one another and our disagreement was easily resolved. And I discovered that our relationship from that point forward was profoundly deepened and greatly enriched.

Looking back, I recognized the dynamics that had perverted my imagination so that I was driven to resolve the conflict with a strategy designed to destroy. My imagination is naturally shaped by the logic of this present evil age. I should have regarded my thoughts and feelings with suspicion, examining them to see if they represented the truth, whether they were shaped by the cross. After all, I tend to want to preserve my dignity and honor, to gain leverage in relationships out of self-preservation. But the cross calls me to die to these desires and to give away any and all leverage. Cruciform postures demand that I put myself into the hands of others, which feels very risky. After all, if I open myself up to others, they may actually do me harm! They may feel very satisfied to leave me on my cross, perhaps even mocking me as onlookers did to Jesus. But I must hold fast to the knowledge that leaving the cross eliminates all possibility that God will work in the situation with resurrection power. Not only will I be on my own, but I will be putting myself squarely within the domain of the present evil age and will be left to the dynamics of the destructive apocalyptic power alliance. Only destruction can flow from that.

I have come to see that when resurrection power is being unleashed in a situation, it liberates and lightens the hearts of everyone involved. It creates space and freedom of movement, rather than pressure and a feeling of being constricted and controlled. When we are shaped by the cross, God's Spirit opens our eyes to creatively imagine endless pathways of redemption that we may take together out of the situation. Cruciformity does not argue its case or seek to prove another person wrong. Rather, it entails a posture of invitation, asking strategic questions, such as, "I understand that thus and so happened, can you help me understand how you see it?" Rather than seeking to corner someone, which is a power move, I can create a safe situation for others that will allow them to feel free to work with me toward resolution.

A Cruciform Expectation of Hope in the Church

Cruciformity holds the promise of orienting pastors toward a posture of receptivity from their churches. Contemporary visions of church leadership tend to situate pastors with their backs to the church as they look ahead to lead the way. Alternatively, pastors may see themselves as situated over and above their churches, imposing their personality and ministry vision on community life. Paul casts a very different vision. He knew Scripture commanded a king in Israel to avoid "exalting himself above other members of the community" (Deut. 17:20). When Paul anticipated visiting the Roman churches, he situated himself rhetorically alongside them, looking to impart a spiritual gift to them and longing to be blessed by them, as well (Rom. 1:11–12). Pastors have important roles to play in shepherding churches, but they also are people loved by God and whom God wants to love, bless, and refresh through the church.

This insight came to me during a season of conflict in our church when I noticed that various leaders were closing themselves off from each other. We were all burned out and tired, and we began to see each other as problems to be solved. Various factions were trying to impose their designs on the church's vision and direction. As I pondered these dynamics on a long walk one day, I was struck by the realization that what we needed to do was to see that we were all God's great gifts to each other. Rather than seeking to assert dominance over each other, we needed to see one another as eternally rich gifts. And this posture needed to start with me. I realized that God loved me so much that he had put Bob and Rebecca and Linda and John and Marlena and Jeffrey in my life. These were not competitors, but friends with infinite gifts to give me and rich sources of refreshment and blessing. This completely changed my posture toward our gatherings and how I saw our community.

We each tend to notice what is wrong with our churches. The people are disappointing, our programs are not exciting, and there is a lack of energy in our leaders. When we see things from this perspective, however, we are adopting postures of power—we are judges noting all the shortcomings in others.

If, however, we take a posture of weakness and humility, we no longer see the church as problematic. Rather than focusing on faults, we can place ourselves in a posture of reception, envisioning the church as God's greatest gift to us. This is how I now approach the church. It is God's gift to me, and I have embarked on a lifelong mission of discovering just how this collection of ordinary and apparently unremarkable people is God's great gift. It is not my responsibility to fix the church or sort anyone else out, but rather I have the opportunity to unwrap God's gifts and receive others as God's goodness to me over the course of a lifetime.

I now go to church with the anticipation of being blessed. I can focus on enjoying one or two conversations in which someone will share with me how their week went. Or, perhaps I will have the opportunity to share with them how things are going with me. Other people with whom I am in community are now potentially rich friends, agents of God's lovingkindness in my life. Cruciformity shapes me to receive the richness that others offer me, so long as I remain in that posture of weakness, humility, and receptivity. I am now oriented toward my church by hopeful expectation of goodness.

These sorts of cruciform postures for participating in the life of God's people are not merely good ideas or wise counsel for ministry. They stir up and radiate the life-giving power of God in Christ by the Spirit. Alternative modes of relating are devastating, for they stir up and radiate the presence of destructive cosmic powers whose aims are division and the destruction of the church of Jesus Christ. It is imperative, then, that we cultivate behaviors of joy and purposeful delight in the church, rather than approaches oriented by power and control.

5

Cruciform Ministry and Image Maintenance

We have considered how the dramatic reversal in Paul's thinking about resurrection realities affected his conception of his ministry. Paul's imagination was transformed with regard to his entire outlook. In this chapter, we will meditate on how this radical renovation in Paul's vision affected his conception of the dynamics associated with image maintenance.

It is crucial for us to reflect on these since we live in a culture dominated by the pursuit of image cultivation and image maintenance. In the late 1980s and early 1990s, the former tennis player André Agassi participated in an advertising campaign organized around the theme, "Image is Everything." He was shown in various poses and postures, looking at times defiant and at others indifferent. One image portrayed him aggressively smacking tennis balls in the desert with his hair flying wildly, and in another he was looking into the distance while sitting on the hood of a Lamborghini. Interestingly, in a memoir that is revelatory and insightful, Agassi admitted that he had worn wigs and had hated that ad campaign.[1]

Image construction certainly did not begin in the 1980s. Modern marketing has dominated contemporary American life for at least the last century, and dynamics related to marketing products have now invaded each of our lives as social media encourage each of us to be

1. André Agassi, *Open: An Autobiography* (New York: Vintage Books, 2010).

our own marketers.[2] While the overt promise of online social media is to connect us to one another, encourage friendship, and foster relationships, one of the unintended effects is to generate a situation in which we each cultivate our "brand," displaying our lives for public consumption in hopes of earning social approval in the form of "likes," "follows," and "mentions." Social media shape us so that we all live as if image is everything.

It may initially sound odd, but Paul knew about social media and image cultivation. While the social medium with which Paul was most familiar was letter writing, this medium for relating socially stirred up the same relational dynamics that orient our lives today. Many of the audiences that received a letter from a Christian leader knew him only from a distance and only encountered the letter and the representative who carried it and read it aloud to the churches that the leader addressed. Since audiences did not have immediate access to that person's faults, failings, quirks, and missteps, it would be easy for him to cultivate an image of lofty spirituality and unique godliness that would set him apart from the rest of the rabble.

Falling Prey to an Image: Galatians

Paul chides the Galatians for giving in to these dynamics. In Galatians 2:1–10, he recounts some of the details of his relationship with the Jerusalem church leaders over the previous decade and a half. In doing so, he speaks of a meeting he had with them, but he does not refer to the Jerusalem leaders in a complimentary way. He speaks of them with various expressions using the Greek verb *dokeō* ("to seem, to appear"). He calls them "those who seem" (*tois dokousin*) in v. 2, "those who seem to be something" (*tōn dokountōn einai ti*) and "those who seem" (*hoi dokountes*) in v. 6, and "those who seem to be pillars" (*hoi dokountes styloi einai*) in v. 9. Between the two uses of *dokeō* in

---

2. For a fascinating review of the rise of modern marketing and its effects on American culture, see Daniel J. Boorstin's classic work, *The Image: A Guide to Pseudo-Events in America* (New York: Vintage, 1992).

verse 6, Paul sarcastically remarks, "what they actually were makes no difference to me; God shows no partiality." The Greek expression for God's impartiality stresses the character of appearances: "the face of a person God does not receive" (*prosōpon ho theos anthrōpou ou lambanei*). That is, none of the ways that people measure one another matters to God. Whatever a person's lofty social status, however impressive a person's accomplishments or fame, God sees a person for who she or he truly is.

Those who were convincing the Galatians to reject Paul's teaching were doing so partly because they had convinced the Galatians that they would be following the Jerusalem apostles and elders. Now, these are people with serious prestige in the early Christian movement. Peter and John were charismatic leaders, as well as physically imposing, and James was the singular leader of the Jerusalem church, the one that all other Christian communities looked to for direction. Perhaps the teachers who had arrived in Galatia after Paul had left were relaying stories of the miracles performed through Peter and John and the strong leadership of James. Their association with these "pillars" gave their teaching credibility and they began to win the loyalty of the Galatians. Because the Galatians only knew the Jerusalem leaders from afar and by reputation from the reports of the Jewish Christian teachers that had come to town, the Galatians were easily led to believe the best about the Jerusalem leaders. They may have seen them as exalted based on their having been followers of Jesus from the very beginning—unlike Paul, who was an early opponent of the church.

In the impressive light of the "pillars" of the church, Paul seemed insignificant. Worse, he was in a position of serious social weakness. When he had passed through Galatia previously, the Galatians had to care for him and nurse him back to health. He had just been stoned in Lystra (cf. Acts 14:19–20), and he and his ministry team needed to just settle somewhere so that Paul could heal and be restored to health. This was the occasion for the founding of the churches in that region. Far from appearing ("seeming") impressive, he actually appeared hideous, with awful wounds that needed bandaging. He notes in Galatians 4:14 that his physical condition during his first visit "put you to the test," indicating that he was in bad shape. He had no capacity to present a polished image of competence and strong leadership.

The reality was that they knew Paul. They had seen him at his weakest and most vulnerable. But they had never met Peter, James, and John, and they only knew these figures by reputation. That is, they were only familiar with their *image*—the conception of these figures fostered by the newly-arrived Jewish Christian teachers. The Galatians only knew what the Jerusalem pillars "seemed" to be. They knew the reputation, but not the reality.

Paul is not denigrating the Jerusalem apostles and elders, nor criticizing them. He is, rather, rebuking the Galatians for holding these men in high esteem with a certain kind of reverence when they did not know them personally. The Galatians wanted to be associated +　with substantial people, with those who seemed to be important; this was causing them to consider taking a terribly destructive step.

✗　Pastors in our day are subject to the same temptation the Galatians faced. The dynamics of Christian celebrity are powerful. Pastors receive an endless stream of offers to attend conferences, listen to speakers, and buy books by "successful" ministry practitioners who seem to have it all figured out, or who promise to equip them with that missing ingredient to take their ministries "to the next level." These dynamics—driven by well-concealed profit motives—produce people "who seem to be something," and we find ourselves elevating such people in our imaginations. We think of them as somehow having the secret to ministry success, or perhaps they are personally gifted in ways that make us feel inadequate to the ministry task. We idealize them as exempt from the ministry struggles that we face. Surely their days are not consumed with the mundane tasks that the rest of us have to deal with!

Paul rejected this approach to his ministry. In recalling his initial presence among the Galatians, he did not try to put a positive spin on his physical condition in an effort to show that he was also an impressive or significant person. On the contrary, Paul was not ashamed to point out the awful physical shape he was in when he first visited them. He refers to his first visit as an opportunity for the Galatians to have seen a public exhibition of Jesus Christ crucified (Gal. 3:1). His repulsive physical condition that had put them to the test was their opportunity to gaze visibly on the battered and expiring corpse of Jesus Christ hanging on the cross. And Paul does not fear speaking so plainly about his condition because his imagination has already been reshaped by the death-life dynamic—humiliation leads to exaltation. Just as God raised Jesus from the dead with resurrection power, God had poured out miracle-working power in Galatia when they saw Paul in that awful shape.

Paul put himself fully before the Galatians without reservation and was unafraid to speak of his humiliation, his vulnerability, and his weakness. This is quite different from how the teachers from Jerusalem were treating them. Paul notes that they "exclude you, so that you may make much of them" (Gal. 4:17). That is, they were manipulating and playing games with the Galatians, insisting that these gentile converts were inferior and that they had something that the Galatians needed. This was the way the visiting teachers built credibility, by making the Galatians feel inadequate, or that they were missing something. Paul concedes that the church does need teachers and it is good for Christians to be equipped for ministry: "It is good to be made much of for a good purpose at all times" (v. 18). But this "making much" of a ministry leader must be done commendably—in relationships of authenticity, vulnerability, and trust, where ministry leaders are not manipulating in order to be well-regarded or gain social status.

For Paul, the ministers who have a legitimate claim to be faithful servants of Christ are those who most closely resemble a corpse on a cross. This is the mindset that drives Paul's understanding of his own apostleship. This is how he interpreted his initial visit to Galatia. He carries "the marks of Jesus branded on my body" (Gal. 6:17). The cultivation of an impressive public image is simply not something Paul was interested in doing. He wanted to be a faithful apostle of Jesus Christ and so cultivated a mode of life that closely resembled the sufferings of Jesus.

Making Much of Ministry Resources

Considering Paul's words regarding "making much" of ministers, he obviously endorsed the notion of looking to others as models for embodying ministry faithfulness. How might we do this in our day, without being taken in by the deceptive dynamics of publicity and marketing? How can we avoid falling prey to the dynamics of our culture's image-orientation so that we fully benefit from the gifts God has given to the church?

First, we can learn from teachers who are honest about their struggles in striving for ministry faithfulness in their particular contexts. Pastors who write about the development of their ministries want to encourage others with hope in the gospel and to persevere in ministry. But in relaying their own histories through anecdotes, they are inevitably selective, may neglect to mention mistakes they have made, and may not mention setbacks, frustrations, and failures. Seek to draw wisdom from those who are honest about their shortcomings, who narrate frankly how they have worked through the temptations and idolatries that affect contemporary church ministry. Look for those who emphasize their need of others, how they have identified their own aims and ambitions as the source of trouble, and how they overcame these.

Second, consider Paul's characterization of the teachers in Galatia as those who "exclude you so that you will make much of them." Beware of teachers and resources that make you feel that you do not have what it takes to experience God's blessing in ministry. If you are made to feel inadequate unless you purchase their resource or implement their growth strategy, set it aside and move on. Look for resources that will encourage you to envision the people in your church as loved by God and as the source of great blessing for you. Gravitate toward books by teachers that make Scripture make sense and that portray ministry as a difficult but joyful task.

Third, as we will discuss below, Paul acknowledges that selective details about someone who is known from a distance may lead to false impressions (cf. 2 Cor. 12:6). Keep in mind, then, that you do not really know the people whose books you read and whose resources you enjoy. In the end, if you really got to know them, you would be unimpressed. No one lives up to their hype. Every faithful minister has difficulty, faces struggles, and feels inadequate to the task.

Finally, learn the most from the ministry practitioners you know the best. Because we see well-known people from afar, our knowledge of them is *mediated*: literally, *we know them through media*. We do not get to see them as they really are, but only as they are presented to us. We are much better off getting to know faithful ministers in person, through time spent in extended conversation, and through various seasons of life and ministry. Regard ministry counsel from those you know well as far more important than wisdom gained from afar. You do not really know whether someone you do not really know is implementing what they say in their lives and ministries.

Fostering an Image in Ministry: 2 Corinthians

While Paul rebukes the Galatians for falling prey to images, he speaks about cultivating an image in 2 Corinthians 10–13. In this final section of the letter, Paul addresses the other side of the image dynamic. The community has come under the influence of some rival teachers who are very impressive and who are presenting themselves as far more credentialed than Paul. He responds by not being too surprised about this since this is how Satan himself deceives people, disguising himself "as an angel of light" (11:14). The deceitfulness of evil is that it plays to human desires for prominence and the desire to be associated with something significant, substantial, desirable, and impressive. This is, after all, the fundamental character of modern advertising. Marketers do not merely portray certain products as attractive and desirable. Rather, they associate their products with a desirable image—an impressive and apparently substantial way of being characterized by prestige, affluence, and success. And since we all want to be admired and envied, we will consider buying whatever product is on offer.

Paul, in contrast to these rival teachers, resolves not to give in to the pressure to compare himself with other ministers: "We do not

dare to classify or compare ourselves with some of those who commend themselves" (2 Cor. 10:12). It is instructive to consider some
aspects of Paul's response to the Corinthians in chapters 10–13. First,
in 10:13–17 Paul states that he will not boast "beyond limits." He will
not speak more profusely and expansively about his ministry than is
really true, portraying his skillfulness as greater than it really is. Paul's
opponents in Corinth were self-promoters (v. 18) who also boasted in
the ministry successes of others (v. 15), since their ultimate aim was
to present themselves to the Corinthians as impressive people. Paul,
however, only talks about his sphere of ministry, what he is called to
do and what he has done. He is not interested in anything else, since
it is not the Corinthians who will judge him, nor anyone else in any
other ministry arena. God himself will judge, and he is the one who
sees through all social image construction to the heart of who we truly
are (v. 18). Since God will judge, Paul resolves to boast in the Lord and
refrain from image construction (i.e., "boasting").

Second, Paul chose to boast about "the things that show my weakness" (11:30), which he repeats in 12:5. That is, his image construction
has to do with portraying how *unimpressive* he is. Paul's credentials
as a faithful minister of Christ are not his great ministry successes,
his impressive resume, or the effect he can have on audiences. On
the contrary, he maintains that his credentials are his sufferings for
Christ, which he lists in 11:23–33. He initiates this section by revealing
that he is tortured by talking about himself and his qualifications. He
does not want to be "boasting" at all, but because the Corinthians are
following leaders that will bring them harm, he is willing to do this.
But he admits that he is "talking like a madman" by arguing that he is
a more faithful minister of Christ than them (v. 23):

> Are they ministers of Christ? I am talking like a madman—I am
> a better one: with far greater labors, far more imprisonments,
> with countless floggings, and often near death. Five times I have
> received from the Jews the forty lashes minus one. Three times I
> was beaten with rods. Once I received a stoning. Three times I was
> shipwrecked; for a night and a day I was adrift at sea; on frequent

journeys, in danger from rivers, danger from bandits, danger from my own people, danger from Gentiles, danger in the city, danger in the wilderness, danger at sea, danger from false brothers and sisters; in toil and hardship, through many a sleepless night, hungry and thirsty, often without food, cold and naked. And, besides other things, I am under daily pressure because of my anxiety for all the churches. Who is weak, and I am not weak? Who is made to stumble, and I am not indignant? (2 Cor. 11:23–29)

Paul continues to dramatically present his ultimate argument for his authenticity as an apostle in vv. 30–33. This is a nearly carnivalesque argument, with Paul swearing in solemn fashion before giving his ultimate credential, which, in light of the impressive-sounding credentials of the "super-apostles," is a joke:

The God and Father of the Lord Jesus (blessed be he forever!) knows that I do not lie. In Damascus, the governor under King Aretas guarded the city of Damascus in order to seize me, but I was let down in a basket through a window in the wall, and escaped from his hands. (2 Cor. 11:31–33)

This is as pathetic as it is crazy. Paul's ultimate credential as a faithful apostle is that he was reduced to being lowered over a city wall in a basket in order to escape with his life. A remarkable admission, when we think in terms of image construction. Paul is purposely avoiding impressive images and portrays himself as one who is faithful to the point where he has had to flee. He is weak. He is vulnerable. He does not portray himself as super-competent and powerful.

Third, Paul has resolved not to use the social medium of letters to cultivate an image (12:6). He has been resisting "boasting" throughout this section of 2 Corinthians, and here he discusses his reasoning: "But if I wish to boast, I will not be a fool, for I will be speaking the truth. *But I refrain from it, so that no one may think better of me* *than what is seen in me or heard from me*" (12:6, emphasis added). Paul knows that he could tell the Corinthians the truth about himself, and that would certainly be impressive. After all, he could tell them about his journeys to heaven and other powerful spiritual experiences. He would also be telling the truth, unlike his opponents in Corinth. But he does not want to speak of these great experiences because he does not want to cultivate that image—to have his life interpreted in that light. He does not want these experiences to be the lens through which they know him. Contrary to the André Agassi ad campaign, Paul knows that *image* is not everything. In fact, even when the truth itself is impressive, it is not something that should be used to construct an image for others to see.

Paul reveals two reasons why he does not go down this road. First, as he says in v. 6, he does not want anyone to think better of him than what is truly the case. Paul knows himself and knows his brokenness and his failings. He also knows the ways that God has gifted him and how he is a blessing to the church of Jesus Christ. But that does not mean he is always easy to live with, and that does not mean he does not have personal failings. Paul is like everyone else. Yes, he has a unique commission in God's overall saving work, but he is a disciple of Jesus Christ who is in need of others and in need of grace. Those who spent significant time around Paul knew him. But with the distance of a letter, it would be easy to hear a few details about his life and have a vision of him as larger than life. These true details could end up constructing an image that is false.

Ministry settings are ripe for these sorts of dynamics. Pastors can project an image through the construction of a church website and use of social media that may have points of contact with what is really true, but they may end up signaling to others an image that extends beyond the truth. Pastors, like anyone else, are real people, with real struggles and failings, and their lives are filled with lots of mundane activities. It is also true that many pastors long to cultivate authenticity and vulnerability. But the dynamics of image cultivation are always at work to seduce us into constructing an image for others in our churches and the wider public. What we fail to realize, however, is that such a pursuit marginalizes the power of God and puts us in situations where we are ministering without the power of God at work.

Thinking that we are strengthening our ministries, we are actually cutting off the source of their life and power.

Paul notes that there is a second reason why he does not pursue the construction of an image through the social medium of letters. He knows that God's power is actually unleashed through weakness and not human power. In 2 Corinthians 12:1–4, Paul describes how God had taken him on heavenly journeys, where he saw and heard things that are too difficult to describe. These visions came at a cost, however. A "thorn" was given to Paul so that he would not become boastful and elevate himself above others—"a messenger of Satan to torment me, to keep me from being too elated" (v. 7). While there has been endless speculation about what this "thorn" might have been, there is no way to know definitively. We can be sure, however, that this must have been very difficult for him. Whatever it was, whether a person harassing his ministry or a physical malady, it caused Paul tremendous stress and anxiety. He reports that he prayed to God three times that it would be taken away, but the answer he received from God was, "My grace is sufficient for you, for power is made perfect in weakness" (v. 9). Because of the reality of cruciformity, it is weakness that draws upon God's power. The cultivation of a powerful image, therefore, eliminates the possibility of drawing upon divine resources.

This is why Paul repeats for a third time in this section that he will gladly boast of his weaknesses (v. 9)—he will happily construct his image in terms of weakness. Only in this way will the power of Christ dwell in him. He is content, therefore, with weaknesses, insults, hardships, persecutions, and calamities for the sake of Christ: for whenever he is weak, then he is strong (v. 10). Rather than portraying for the Corinthians an impressive image of himself, he cultivates authenticity. He is vulnerable about the shame he has endured and the insults he has suffered for his ministry. For Paul, God's resurrection power is not unleashed through people of high social status or by cultivating an image that is impressive. God pours out resurrection power where there are cruciform postures and conditions. Rather than projecting an impressive and powerful image through a social medium, Paul projected an image of himself as weak, knowing that

God only provides divine power where there is human weakness. Only when Paul is weak, is he strong. The same is true for pastors. ✝ They are strong when they cultivate weakness.

Inhabiting an Image of Weakness

Knowing the dynamics of image construction and image maintenance, Paul purposely cultivated an image of weakness. He "boasted" of his weaknesses, making them his calling card and the lens through which the Corinthians viewed him. How might ministry practitioners follow Paul's example in contemporary ministry contexts? It is not very effective to make superficial changes, such as saying, "well, I'm not really a pastor, but just an average Christian." If that is my position, this is misleading and does not really get at the subtler ways we project power. There are endless ways of inhabiting weakness more faithfully, and here are some suggestions.

Interrogating Hopes and Fears

⚔ Prayerfully reflect on how you hope to be seen by others, and make an inventory of how you want to be perceived. Seek to determine the underlying dynamics, the subterranean motivations that lie hidden beneath these desires. How do you want others to see you as "strong," and why? You can also ask yourself about your fears. What are you afraid of when it comes to others' perception of you? What is the worst thing, when it comes to your public persona? And why is this so? What are the weaknesses that you hope no one detects?

This is difficult work. It is not easy to confront our fears and to honestly identify our hopes for how others will perceive us. But it is necessary work if we want to imitate Paul's quest to embody an image of weakness in order to be truly strong. We actually have great resources in our lives to help us in this project: a spouse, our children, and our close ministry associates. We can invite them into this effort and ask them to help us identify ways that we want to be seen. And here is a warning from personal experience: if you ask others to be honest with you, they very well may! Biblical wisdom, however, tells us that such "wounds" from friends in the form of honest feedback are life-giving gifts (Prov. 27:6).

Once you have identified these hopes for how you are perceived, along with how you typically hide your weaknesses, you can reflect on how you can inhabit those weaknesses and make them the markers of your identity. Here is an example of what I have done as a seminary professor. I know that I want to be seen as competent and I hate it when a student asks a question for which I do not have a good answer. I am very uncomfortable with having my inadequacies exposed in the classroom. After some reflection on this inner dynamic, I decided I would begin to posture myself in my classes as the "lead student." I begin every semester by insisting that my students do not call me "Dr. Gombis," but address me by my first name. I cheerfully tell them that I am a "useless doctor," one that knows a lot but cannot do anything useful if someone is choking in a restaurant or faints on an airplane. I posture myself as their partner in the task of ministry preparation, so I would much rather be called "Tim."

I also tell them that I teach New Testament in seminary for my own purposes of growth, and that they are responsible to ask good questions and provoke me to reflect on where I need to learn. This strategy for inhabiting weakness is so liberating for me because it releases me from having to portray myself as ultra-competent, hiding my weaknesses and responding with dishonest bluster when someone asks a question that exposes my ignorance.

If I were in a ministry context, I might want others to see me as a decisive leader, projecting confidence in my decisions. Underlying this may be a fear that others will see me as weak and indecisive. I would likely justify this by saying that people need to see their pastor as competent, one who knows the will of God for God's people. After all, we usually express our hopes and fears for how others will see us in spiritual language in order to justify them. We need to break through the nicely dressed-up self-deceptions in order to expose our true motivations.

To inhabit an image of weakness, I would consider the following approach to a staff meeting.

Okay folks, a moment of honesty: regarding the situation we are facing, I think I have arrived at the best way forward and here is where you probably are ready for me to weigh in and make a decision. But I'm working on some inner dynamics related to my hopes and fears about how I am perceived as a leader and pastor of this church. I don't like projecting an image of uncertainty and I want you all to see me as decisive. Here is what I think we should do. I know, however, that my idea may need to be refined or questioned and that your thoughts and objections would either lead us to a more fruitful course of action or modify my idea so that it leads to greater blessing. I would love to hear your thoughts.

We may feel that we build the trust of others when we portray strength, but inviting others into decision-making processes often is more effective in earning the trust of others.

Reflecting on the Dynamics of Cruciformity

Reflecting on the dynamics of cruciformity can also reveal possibilities for inhabiting an image of weakness. The cross is the site of resurrection power and wherever people inhabit cruciform postures and relational practices, God pours out resurrection life that liberates, gives life, and creates joy. Cruciformity sets others in a place where they feel they have space to move and are free to be themselves. Knowing this, and perhaps explaining this to others, you can inquire of your staff and ministry leaders—along with family members—where your presence is liberating and life-giving, and where others feel constrained and conflicted. What habits do you have that shut others down? What dynamics are involved when others feel they are not free to be honest with you, or speak their mind?

Taking this step will feel very threatening, but it has the promise of unleashing unspeakable blessing into your relationships. These are great opportunities to see where and how you can inhabit an image of weakness.

I might have a staff person reveal to me that occasionally I make passive-aggressive comments that provoke confusion and resentment in others. It shuts them down and closes off conversation, causing others to walk on eggshells around me. I will need to reflect on why I do this and learn to speak my mind more plainly and in ways that open others up, giving them freedom and life. As a way of inhabiting an image of weakness that paradoxically makes me strong, I might identify myself as a recovering passive-aggressive communicator. Owning that identity would be a strategically powerful way to overcome being passive-aggressive! Being explicit about that weakness and the desire to grow in that way would lighten the atmosphere around you, liberating others to inhabit joy around you and to be themselves. Honestly identifying that weakness and making it your calling card—your "boast"—is a creative way to draw upon resurrection power. That is creatively being strong by inhabiting weakness.

Exploiting Worldly Leadership Advice

A great way to creatively come up with ways to inhabit and embody an image of weakness is to investigate literature from business books on how to project an image of strength, prestige and power. For example, I once heard that one way to establish dominance over a colleague, or to reinforce to a subordinate that a power differential exists, is to purposely get their name wrong. Someone actually did this to me one time. Because I knew that this person occasionally played manipulative games in his relationships, I suspected it was intentional. Whether or not it was, it was helpful for me to reflect on how diminished I felt; how I felt taken aback and shut down, put in my place.

Learning practices whereby people reinforce power dynamics is a great way to learn more about how realities work. It is also a wonderful way to think creatively about how to embody the opposite sort of practices, ones that project dignity onto others, behaviors that invite others in, opening them up and giving them life. I reflected on the interchange I just mentioned when I began my teaching career. I had several Bible classes that had at least eighty students in them, but I committed myself to learning each of their names every semester.

I was helped by the fact that we could print out rosters with student pictures on them. I quizzed myself over their names each day when I arrived in my office so that when I bumped into them in the hallway or the cafeteria, their name would be on the tip of my tongue. I cannot recount how many times just saying someone's name made them feel valued and radiated to them significance. It was one way for me to resist the temptation to play power games, and to strategically inhabit weakness. There are endless possibilities for embodying postures of weakness so that the resurrection power of God is unleashed into our lives and radiated to others.

6

Cruciformity and Credential Accumulation

Like anyone else, pastors struggle with feelings of inadequacy. Caring for God's people is an overwhelming task, which may drive ministers to look for something that will make them feel up to it. They may pursue education to help them deal with the challenges they face. Some may seek to alleviate a perceived lack by acquiring a credential that gives them a certain status, granting them the credibility and confidence they need to lead people. Credentials can become problematic, however, when they are used to construct an identity that makes one "worthy" of ministering in the church, or when they become part of an effort to establish a social identity—especially if pastors imagine this identity is how God sees them. Before his conversion, Paul had been wrapped up in a pursuit of socially impressive credentials in order to build a personal status that would enable him to stake a claim for resurrection at the day of the Lord.

Paul's Former Pursuit of Credentials

In Philippians 3, Paul writes about his transformed conception of his credentials. He tells his audience that "it is we who are the circumcision" (v. 3), indicating that they are the true people of God. They "worship in the Spirit of God and boast in Christ Jesus and have no confidence in the flesh" (v. 3). The expression, "no confidence in the flesh," indicates that the basis upon which Christians know they are God's people has nothing at all to do with their worldly identities. Paul is making a specific reference to their confidence that they will be claimed by God at the final day of salvation and judgment—the day of Christ. It does not matter that they may be rich or poor, male or female, slave or free, Greek, Jewish or whatever else. They do not put confidence in any of these earthly identity markers for their acceptance before God.

Their "boast" is in their identity as a people gathered by Jesus Christ. That is their calling card, their reason for being, the reality of who they are and what gives them value. They do not assemble according to their shared social class, or ethnicity, or because they have any other earthly identity in common, but only because they all confess an allegiance to the reigning Lord Jesus. This would have been an unprecedented reality in the ancient world. Guilds of artisans gathered together, clubs of the same social class met for dinners, and people assembled in households according to a shared family identity. But the church community met together and shared in a meal to perform and embody their common identity in their relation to Jesus Christ. Christian identity before others and human identity before God is shaped by owning one's participation among the people of Jesus Christ. To have any other indicator of value before others and before God is "putting confidence in the flesh"—it is the cultivation of a worldly identity in order to be acceptable to God.

If Paul was such a person to put confidence in the flesh, he would have great reason for doing so, as he states in v. 4. According to social conventions of his inherited culture, he had constructed the ideal identity for establishing an honored place among the people of God. He could be confident that he would be saved at the day of resurrection because he had an impressive list of credentials:

> If anyone else has reason to be confident in the flesh, I have more: circumcised on the eighth day, a member of the people of Israel, of the tribe of Benjamin, a Hebrew born of Hebrews; as to the law, a Pharisee; as to zeal, a persecutor of the church; as to righteousness under the law, blameless. (Phil. 3:4–6)

Paul had been born into the historic people of God—he was an Israelite, a Hebrew born to Hebrew parents, having been circumcised on the eighth day, in accordance with biblical commandment (Lev. 12:3). His devotion to the Mosaic law was manifest in that he had trained as a Pharisee. Not only was he a teacher of Torah to God's people, but he was a member in good standing of the group that was passionately praying for and working to bring about resurrection life for Israel.

As far as zeal for God and for the purity of God's people was concerned, he had been a persecutor of the church. He had spent his career in zealously purging impurity and worldly elements from among the Jewish people. And he had achieved the status of a "righteous" man, blamelessly living in accordance with the law.

These credentials set Paul at the very center of his people, occupying an impressive and exalted social status. He had checked all the boxes and had become an esteemed person in terms that were set according to how they read Scripture. He had inherited a spotless cultural identity and had built up a personal reputation that earned him praise from his peers. He was someone to be given attention, reverence, and honor. When it came to the salvation of God's people at the anticipated day of the Lord, Paul assumed that he would be at the head of the line.

Before his conversion, however, Paul would not have stated that his confidence was "in the flesh." He would have thought that his confidence was in God and in God's word. After all, he saw himself as a faithful Israelite. He was honoring Torah and serving the one true God! He imagined that he was boasting in God and hoping in God's approval of those who are faithful and who zealously pursue the truth. He was unaware that he had made his "boast"—his calling card and his identity—a set of credentials that were utterly irrelevant regarding God's purposes and that would be meaningless at the day of Christ.

After hearing from the exalted Lord Jesus on the way to Damascus, Paul's self-conception was radically altered, as we have already discussed. He saw that his entire pursuit was oriented by the present evil age. Because God vindicated the one Paul considered "unrighteous," and "accursed by God," all of his credentials were now worse than irrelevant (as we will discuss below). Far from his having confidence in the God of Israel, Paul realized that his confidence was "in the flesh," the realm of sinful humanity that is thoroughly corrupt.

Modern Temptations to Build Credentials

The dynamics of Paul's credential-building agenda have great relevance for contemporary ministry. Paul associated his well-cultivated and immaculate social value with how God would have perceived him. That is, he assumed that God was just as impressed with his status and achievements as everyone else in his culture. Just like Paul, we tend to associate these horizontal and vertical dimensions of our self-perceived value. It is helpful, then, to reflect on the ways that contemporary ministers establish their value through credential-building, and how the assumption subtly works its way into our imaginations that our social credentials establish our status before God.

One of the ways that contemporary pastors construct their social identity—the credential that signals their value—is the size of their churches. A variety of values in our culture encourage ministers to evaluate the health of their churches by how much the church is growing numerically. I've seen this happen hundreds of times: when pastors gather at conferences, the first question they ask each other is, "How big is your church?" It's how we measure ourselves against one another. This is one of the ways that thinking about the economy or the housing market affects how we envision ministry. A strong country has a growing economy. A healthy economy has a growing housing market. Therefore, a good pastor must be one who has a big and growing church. Because our imaginations are shaped by these economic indicators, I will feel good about myself if my church is bigger than someone else's. And I'll feel badly about myself and my ministry if I run into a pastor whose church is bigger.

Another ministerial credential-building route is the accumulation of academic degrees, preferably from a prestigious seminary. Pastors with an MA degree in ministry may feel inferior to pastors with an MDiv, the standard degree that seminaries offer. Conversely, pastors with a doctoral degree—a DMin or PhD—may feel that they rank in superiority over those with only an MA. I knew a pastor who never tired of reminding his church about his seminary education and just what seminary he attended. This was such an important part of his self-conception.

Seminaries market their degrees with the promise that earning one will equip pastors with the skills they need to meet the challenges of their ministries and the complexities of our cultural context. The message is subtly hidden within such marketing strategies that if a pastor were to earn an advanced degree, they would have a credential that establishes them as having a status that has greater value than if they otherwise did not have that degree.

A further window into the drive for credential-building is to pay attention to the introductions of well-known pastors when they speak at ministry conferences. Advertisements for conferences include biographies of pastors who speak in such settings. Very seldom do these listings refer to the sort of things we find in Paul's letters regarding the character of elders and pastors. In the Pastoral Letters (1–2 Timothy, Titus), Paul speaks of not being pugnacious, of being free from the love of money, and of being hospitable. But ministry conference advertisements rarely make mention of such practices and virtues like contentment or marital faithfulness. Rather, they include their academic degrees and the sizes of their churches. This reflects and reinforces the values by which we measure ministers. Certain pastors "matter" because of their credentialization in terms of academics and books published. They are important and people should listen to them because their church is large.

These dynamics create in other pastors the desire to accumulate similar credentials. The message is clearly delivered to younger ministers: "You will have value if you pursue an academic degree. You will have significance before others—and will be an approved minister before God—if your church is growing, or has a large congregation."

This leads to another credential that ministers are drawn to achieve: speaking at ministry conferences. I talked recently with a young woman training for ministry and asked her about her ministry goals. She said she was hoping to be a conference speaker. She spoke frankly about wanting to "have an impact." Our contemporary reality of the conference circuit creates these aspirations. We even have terms that reflect and generate these dynamics, such as "thought leader," or "person of influence." Advertisements also reflect these credentials: "She has spoken to thousands of pastors at conferences."

I had a conversation about these dynamics with a few ministry friends, and Brenda (one of a few local pastors who is also a very gifted musician) mentioned that another way pastors establish an impressive credential is by associating themselves with well-known artists and performers. These might be popular church musicians or artists with large followings in the wider culture. We are all aware of the dynamics and practices of "name-droppers," who seek an exalted social status based on whom they know and to whom they are connected, however tenuously.

The following questions may provide some help in identifying the dynamics of credentialization that affect how we see ourselves:

- Why am I fit to be a pastor or ministry leader? What qualifies me?
- Why am I adequate to be the pastor of this church, or leader of this ministry?
- What is my calling card?
- When I speak with other pastors, what do I want them to know about me and my ministry?
- Why should the people in my ministry listen to me?
- How do I measure how well things are going in my ministry?
- If I never am asked to speak at a ministry conference, can I still perceive that I am a successful minister?
- If my church or ministry never grows numerically, can I still be happy and content as a minister?

Credentials and Cruciformity

Paul goes on in Philippians 3 to discuss the transformation of his credential-building program:

Yet whatever gains I had, these I have come to regard as loss be- ✗
cause of Christ. More than that, I regard everything as loss because of the surpassing value of knowing Christ Jesus my Lord.
For his sake I have suffered the loss of all things, and I regard them
as rubbish, in order that I may gain Christ and be found in him,
not having a righteousness of my own that comes from the law,
but one that comes through faith in Christ, the righteousness
from God based on faith. I want to know Christ and the power
of his resurrection and the sharing of his sufferings by becoming
like him in his death, if somehow I may attain the resurrection
from the dead. (Phil. 3:7–11)

The first thing to notice is that Paul now sees his credentials as "loss":
"whatever gains I had, these I have come to regard as loss" (v. 7).
Intensifying his negative regard of his credentials, he now sees them
"as rubbish" (v. 8), which is a very polite translation. The Greek term
refers to excrement (*skybala*), sometimes translated as "trash" (The
Message), "sewer trash" (CEB), "dung" (KJV) or "garbage" (NIV).
Paul obviously saw his former credentials as something odious! It
is not that these inherited and accumulated credentials were bad in
themselves, but for Paul these credentials are now "loss *because of
Christ*" (v. 7). He repeats this comparison twice in v. 8. He regards
all these markers of personal value as "loss *because of* the surpassing
value of knowing Christ Jesus my Lord. *For his sake* I have suffered
the loss" of all the personal attributes that he formerly looked to in
order to establish his personal value.

They are loss because of Christ, for the specific reason that these
credentials now stand in the way of Paul owning the supreme credential of identifying with the socially shameful cruciform Jesus. Paul
realizes that the only credential that matters is having his personal
value and identity thoroughly shaped by the cross. And because of
that, his having a collection of socially and culturally impressive credentials becomes an obstacle, since they still appeal to him to establish his personal value in those terms—his value before others and
before God.

Paul no longer wants to be known and regarded according to his impressive worldly credentials, but to be known and regarded as being "in Christ" instead. When he speaks of "forgetting what lies behind," he is referring specifically to his impressive credentials (v. 13). He now strives to "gain Christ" and to be "found in Christ." That is, he wants to be identified by his location along the downward trajectory of Christ, who did not exploit his identity as God, but rather embarked on a journey of self-expenditure and went to the absolute lowest place of humiliation—death on a cross (Phil. 2:6–8). Rather than exploit his advantages and privileges, he took the form of a servant. As we discussed in chapter 2, this is an absolutely countercultural pursuit and a counterintuitive mode of life that runs against the grain of contemporary ministry strategies of identity construction. This is a way of life that radiates dignity to others through service, seeking to foster their flourishing, driven by the confidence that this is how we enjoy the resurrection power of God.

Paul's position of being "in Christ" is now his singular personal identity marker, and so he aims to live into the fullness of that life of self-expenditure for the sake of others. This entails an active flight from his credentials, a single-minded refusal to be identified with his former prerogatives and accomplishments, since these prevent him from enjoying the socially shameful identity marker of being associated with the cross of Christ. His value before God—his "righteousness"—now comes from being "in Christ," rather than an identity of his own construction, even though he had cultivated that righteousness based on a value system oriented by the Mosaic law (v. 9). That former personal value construction is utterly irrelevant for his current enjoyment of resurrection power and for his future joyful participation in the resurrection at the day of Christ. The only reality that gives him access to experiencing the power of Christ's resurrection now is his being shaped by the cross of Christ (v. 10).

This reality—the enjoyment of resurrection power now and participation in the resurrection in the end—drives Paul's refusal to pursue the accumulation of credentials that would be impressive within his social circles. It also drives his construction of a ministry mode that is thoroughly oriented by the cross. Paul's ultimate credential that establishes the validity of his ministry is his being morphed into the shape of the cross, which involves his participation in the sufferings of Christ.

Paul's Cruciform Credentials in His Letters

We can get a sense of how Paul constructs his credentials for his ministry by surveying the greetings in his letters. This is where Paul identifies himself, establishing his right to address his audiences and carry out his ministry as an apostle. Consistently, Paul identifies his credentials in two related ways: he is called by God, and he is a slave of Jesus Christ.

- Paul, a slave (*doulos*) of Jesus Christ, called to be an apostle, set apart for the gospel of God (Rom. 1:1)
- Paul, called to be an apostle of Christ Jesus by the will of God (1 Cor. 1:1)
- Paul, an apostle of Christ Jesus by the will of God (2 Cor. 1:1)
- Paul an apostle—sent neither by human commission nor from human authorities, but through Jesus Christ and God the Father, who raised him from the dead (Gal. 1:1)
- Paul, an apostle of Christ Jesus by the will of God (Eph. 1:1)
- Paul and Timothy, slaves (*douloi*) of Christ Jesus (Phil. 1:1)
- Paul, an apostle of Christ Jesus by the will of God (Col. 1:1)
- For our appeal does not spring from deceit or impure motives or trickery, but *just as we have been approved by God to be entrusted with the message of the gospel*, even so we speak, not to please mortals, but to please God who tests our hearts. (1 Thess. 2:3–4)
- Paul, an apostle of Christ Jesus by the command of God our Savior and of Christ Jesus our hope (1 Tim. 1:1)
- Paul, an apostle of Christ Jesus by the will of God, for the sake of the promise of life that is in Christ Jesus (2 Tim. 1:1)

- Paul, a slave (*doulos*) of God and an apostle of Jesus Christ (Titus 1:1)
- Paul, a prisoner of Christ Jesus, and Timothy our brother (Philem. 1:1)

We can make a few observations about how Paul constructs his ministry credentials. First, Paul repeatedly notes that he is appointed by God to his position as an apostle. He does not point to anything he has done, nor does he list any impressive credentials. Rather, he ascribes the activity to God. God is the active agent of his appointment to ministry. *Paul is called to this.* This might be read as a power move, and certainly in our day such a move has been abusively made, with deceptive leaders appealing to divine authority to endorse their exploitative treatment of others. But this would be to misread what Paul is doing. In fact, contrary to manipulative leaders, Paul is not setting himself *apart from* or *over* his audiences at all. His rhetorical strategy situates him *alongside* his audiences.

In Romans and 1 Corinthians, Paul notes that he is "called" as an apostle, and just after this, indicates that his audiences are also called. They are called as saints, "holy ones" (Rom. 1:7; 1 Cor. 1:2). Just as he has been appointed by God, they, too, have been appointed by God. In addition, he is a spokesperson for God, indicating to his audiences that he is appointed to direct his audiences how they might enjoy God's presence among them.

The first Thessalonian letter is an exception, though it reinforces this point. Paul does not identify his credential at the start of the letter, but rather mentions his right to address them in the second chapter. He points to God as the one who took the initiative to call Paul to this task, noting that he and his ministry associates "have been approved by God to be entrusted with the message of the gospel" (1 Thess. 2:4). The other exception to this consistent pattern is 2 Thessalonians, in which Paul does not mention a credential. Here, however, he points to his conducting himself as a servant while he was among them (2 Thess. 3:8), which leads to our second point.

In a few places, Paul identifies himself with terminology that situates him in the lowest possible social location. He is a slave (*doulos*) of Jesus Christ. This is one way that Paul can identify with and imitate in his life what Christ did when he "took the form of a slave (*doulos*)" (Phil. 2:7). Slaves in the ancient world had no rights, lacked any social value, and did not technically exist as anything other than property in the eyes of the law. It is a shameful identity marker, but Paul gladly embraces it as his calling card precisely because it identifies him with the lowest possible social location, which allows him to identify intimately with the cruciform Jesus. This is completely different from contemporary ministry pressures to identify with exalted social stations!

Paul does not identify himself with his expertise or his skillfulness. He does not lift himself above his audiences, but addresses them from a posture of mutuality, situating himself alongside them. He identifies his ministry partners as "brothers" (1 Cor. 1:1; Col. 1:1), "fellow workers" (1 Cor. 3:9; Philem. 1, 23), and "fellow slaves" (Col. 1:7). Because of our modern lenses, we may regard Paul as the great apostle, the "senior pastor," the "CEO," or "executive director" of his ministry team, *but that is not how Paul identified himself.* ✗

This makes Paul accountable to God for carrying out his ministry (1 Cor. 4:2–5). And because it situates Paul *alongside* his audiences rather than *over* them, it makes him dependent upon them for carrying out his ministry. In a number of places, he requests prayer from his audiences for faithfulness and effectiveness in his ministry (Rom. 1:12; Eph. 6:19–20; Phil. 1:19).

Contemporary Credentialing for Cruciform Ministry

Paul's example indicates that the fundamental credential for ministers is that they are called by God as servants and responsible caregivers for God's people. Being called by God is wonderfully liberating because our identities are not wrapped up in how people evaluate us. God alone sets the agenda for our service to God's people. Now this does not mean that we may regularly remind people we don't care how they feel about us. Rather, it frees us up to gladly serve the church, loving others, honoring them, and relating to them so that God's grace is always flooding their lives. Inhabiting the same ministry identity as Paul also releases us from the quest to seek further credentials that would somehow demonstrate to others—and to ourselves—that we really are adequate for the tasks of ministry.

There are many ways of practically embodying this, but one suggestion is that pastors and ministry leaders request that people address them by their first name, especially in ministry situations where terms like "pastor" communicate high esteem. As we indicated previously, "pastor" is another term for shepherd, which was a position of low regard in the ancient world. Because of this, the term points to all the tasks associated with responsible care for people in the church, looking after their needs and their spiritual and physical well-being. Unfortunately, contemporary pastoral ministry has become associated with "leadership," which in our current cultural climate suggests someone like a CEO or business executive who is far removed from the common life of the everyday people in our churches. Because Paul situated himself alongside his churches as a "brother," and even underneath them as a "slave," anything we can do to situate ourselves likewise is worth considering.

The same goes for those with doctorates. To insist on being addressed with an academic title runs directly counter to the spirit of Paul's ministry postures. Doing so indicates that we see ourselves as positioned above the people to whom we minister, rather than alongside or underneath.

When pastors speak to others about what is happening in their churches, they can consider using lots of "we" talk, rather than speaking about what "I" am doing. This includes pastors along with their people in initiatives they are pursuing. I had a seminary professor who routinely bristled and interrupted pastors who spoke about "my people," in referring to their churches. He would ask, "*whose* people?" Churches are made up of those called by God, those who belong to God and God alone, people whom pastors are privileged to serve and care for responsibly.

And when pastors address their churches, using anecdotes to illustrate biblical realities, they can consider how to rhetorically situate themselves alongside everyone else as fellow disciples. Are you
always the hero of your stories? Do you portray yourself as one who
routinely does the right thing? We all know that life is not that tidy
and that discipleship is a lot messier than we like to portray. Share
stories in which you learned something, or speak about times you
needed to confess sin or pursue reconciliation after you caused relational tension. Speaking from a position *alongside* others carries with
it a powerful dynamic of invitation that draws others into discipleship
along with you. It portrays Christian discipleship truthfully, and it
rhetorically situates you along with the disciples God has called you
to serve.

These are just a few of the countless ways to develop ministry
credentials that resemble Paul's. I invite you to prayerfully activate
your imagination to explore ways you have fallen into situating yourself above and over others, and to consider how to adopt postures
alongside and underneath.

What Is Seminary Training Good For?

The discussion thus far raises the question of why anyone would go to
seminary in order to prepare for ministry. Considering Paul's former
pursuit, is there any legitimacy to a seminary education? Further, in
light of seminary as "cemetery" jokes that point to the reality that for
some, that's where their faith goes to die, is there any point?

I think there is great value in a seminary education in preparation for faithful ministry to God's people. It is crucial that ministers
develop and continue to sharpen their critical thinking skills. By
"critical," I mean the ability to discern the distance between how my
tradition reads the Bible and the Bible itself. Critical thought also involves the growing awareness that when I read the Bible, I am shaped
to see certain realities and dynamics in the text and to ignore others.
Developing disciplined ways of thinking increases my ability to read
Scripture for what it is saying and not for what I want it to say, or for

what I have been trained to see there. Such an approach to Scripture allows me to hear God's voice clearly and to speak to God's people based on what God has actually said.

Of course, there is always the danger that in developing critical thinking we may develop critical spirits, condescendingly dismissing other people and their viewpoints. While this is something we always need to be on the lookout for, we cannot let this danger keep us from sharpening our skills in handling Scripture and analyzing ourselves and our culture. I tell my students that when we are in the classroom, we are engaging in an intensely critical enterprise, taking a penetrating look into the biblical text and then also discerning how God's vision for God's people is, and is not, being embodied by our churches. But we are only doing this in order to discern how we can strategically embody the love and grace of God in our ministries. When we leave the classroom, we do not necessarily engage in the same conversations with people in our churches. What we are learning at seminary is equipping us to be more skillful hearers of God's word and lovers of God's people. We are not necessarily gaining information that is critical for people in the pew to know. What we learn shapes us as people who can then turn and open up Scripture for the church.

Critical thinking also helps us discern how the corruptions of our surrounding cultures have affected the corporate lives of our churches. There are times when pastors must speak a prophetic word to God's people, and they can be prepared for this in seminary classrooms that discern and discuss how the ideologies and cultural patterns that dominate the present evil age have worked their way into our communities. I'm thinking here of ideologies and cultural practices fostered by the pervasive individualism in our culture, along with approaches to ministry that influence ministry practitioners to imagine themselves as delivering or selling a product to consumers. And this is to say nothing of the gender and racial injustices that orient our communities. These and many other values spawn ways of thinking that shape our corporate practices, and a seminary classroom is an excellent place to analyze the dynamics involved and offer hopeful gospel alternatives.

All of this is to say that a seminary education has great value if it is equipping ministry practitioners with skills in interpreting Scripture and reckoning with how to feed God's people with God's word. Studying biblical languages and developing theological skill and discernment aid pastors in portraying for God's people the wonders of a cross-oriented vision. They can learn to speak about this reality and offer the promise of ever-greater growth in enjoying resurrection life on earth while headed for resurrection at the day of Christ.

So, what is a seminary education good for? It is indeed good, so long as it is fostering a faithfully cruciform ministry vision characterized by joyful service and the cultivation of community dynamics of service and hospitality toward the hurting and the marginalized. A seminary degree should not be sought because it is a credential that promises a successful career or an impressive social status.

Justification by Faith and Cruciform Ministry

The dynamics of credential accumulation are tempting for pastors and ministry practitioners. As I noted at the start of this chapter, most people in ministry struggle with inadequacy—the feeling of being overwhelmed by the tasks, demands on their time, and the pressures on their families. They may not feel up to the job and may sense that there is something out there that will make them more secure in their position, something that will give them a sense of adequacy that finally gives them value. These dynamics generate great anxiety and fear among pastors.

Pastors would do well to give extended consideration to justification by faith, which provides the solution to these anxieties and fears. As an alternative to the quest for socially impressive credentials in order to stake a claim of value before others and to make a claim for resurrection at the final day, Paul wanted to be conformed to the cross of Christ. He wanted to be "found in Christ"—located "in him"—having a righteousness (i.e., a justified status) that would bring about resurrection "through the faithfulness of Christ" (*dia pisteōs Christou*, Phil. 3:9). Paul speaks of his union with Christ in a manner that depicts him being wrapped up into the very faithfulness of Jesus Christ, and that is the cosmic location where God conforms him into the cruciform character of the Son of God. Paul's location in Christ is what determines his identity before God and, therefore, before others.

This provides great liberation and freedom from the pursuit of credentials. Freedom from the anxiety of seeking to establish a claim for value comes only by being conformed to the cross. Paul does not need to boast in any other earthly identity, but only that he is attached to Christ, drawn into the very life of Jesus Christ by the Spirit, a reality that powers Paul's life and ministry. Being so located in the cruciform life-pattern of Christ guarantees that we will arrive at the day of resurrection and enter into the joy of full and final salvation.

Pastors are set free based on their being declared righteous before God to minister from freedom. They do not need to look to any other earthly identity. The temptation to accumulate credentials is an empty pursuit. Once a person achieves a credential and looks to it for value before other people, they will soon feel inadequate for some other reason, and feel the need to pursue yet another credential. They may hear that while they have a doctorate, they are not a conference speaker, or they are not in the inner circle of some famous ministry figure. This endless quest is a fruitless one. If pastors are constantly on the lookout for some further basis on which they might establish their value, they will radiate that insignificance to others, and will minister from a vision of the Christian faith that encourages others to establish their claims for significance based on some elusive pursuit. They will end up betraying the gospel in so doing.

Letting go of this pursuit is not easy, as internal pressures and external messages constantly portray the pursuit of credentials as either necessary or tempting. It is crucial, however, to purposefully enjoy the liberating space of the gospel and to draw others in, by focusing our identities on the wonders of the cross, unleashing the dynamics of resurrection.

7

Cruciformity, Passivity, and Taking the Initiative

When I talk about cruciformity to people in ministry, or to those who are preparing for ministry, I often get questions like this: "Should I just let everyone walk all over me, or treat me like a doormat?" The assumption here seems to be that cruciformity is the same thing as passivity—that embodying the cross of Christ in our ministries entails allowing people to do to us whatever they want without saying anything. Indeed, such a conception of ministry is pretty hopeless.

Cruciformity, however, is anything but passive. On the contrary, cruciformity involves taking the initiative to positively and purposefully conduct one's ministry in such a way that one is stirring up and kicking into gear the dynamics of the cross in the hope of generating resurrection life. As we have discussed in previous chapters, the dynamics of cruciformity involve taking the shape of the cross with the confidence that such postures and relationship dynamics are the only ones upon which God pours out resurrection life and power. This does not involve doing nothing and letting others do what they please. A cruciform ministry will involve at least the following intentionally cultivated practices and dynamics.

Cruciformity and Preaching

A cruciform ministry will involve shaping a church's imagination over time through preaching and teaching the dynamics of cruciformity. The church is the social entity on earth that is claimed by the cross and in which every member owns and claims the cross as their identity. Christian baptism is the act of entry into the church whereby individuals identify publicly with the death and resurrection of Jesus Christ. That is, just as Jesus Christ died to Sin and to this present evil age, rendering God's judgment upon them, and bringing about a new creation in himself, people who are baptized signal their identification with this entire reality. They are saying publicly that they are dead to this world and fully alive in the new creation in Christ by the power of the Holy Spirit. They identify fully with the death of Christ as the reality by which they have their sins forgiven and have the status as "righteous" before God. They also give up their right to insist on their own way, submitting to the lordship of Jesus Christ and committing to living among God's people who are learning to "put on Christ" (Rom. 13:14; cf. Eph. 4:24; Col. 3:10). This involves the cultivation of completely new modes of life characterized by self-giving love, confessing sin to others, and forgiving those who sin against them, along with joyful obedience to the life-giving commands of God in Christ that orient this new life.

Cruciform pastors will routinely and regularly *remind* (literally, recall this reality to everyone's minds) the church of this reality and speak from this reality so that over time this vision of life shapes the corporate imagination of the congregation. This is not something tangential! Rather, it is the central organizing principle of who we are as Christian people gathered in the name of Jesus. The entire New Testament speaks of this from beginning to end, so that pastors can preach about this reality from Matthew to Revelation. In the Gospels, Jesus calls disciples to take up their crosses and to follow him on the road to the cross. Matthew, Mark and Luke tell the story of Jesus's arrival into the world to proclaim the establishment of the kingdom of God, and how Jesus becomes the ruler of that kingdom by being crucified on the cross. John tells the story of how Jesus fully and faithfully reveals God in his death and calls disciples to remain in him by loving one another in the same way that Jesus loved them. The way of life Jesus proclaims in the Gospels is the manner in which the church embodies the cross. God dwells among his people as they enact community patterns shaped by the cross.

When pastors preach and teach about the way of the cross, therefore, they are not speaking about something that is on the periphery of the faith, as if much of Scripture is filled with self-help material or devotional nuggets, and here and there speaks of a cruciform way of life. This reality is central to the Gospels and so preaching on any part of them will involve describing it and pressing it home to the community's corporate imagination.

This is the same way of life described in the book of Acts and, as we have seen in much of this book, in Paul's letters, too. We could go on to describe how this works out in the rest of the New Testament documents, but I hope that the point has already been made. The main way pastors can cultivate a cruciform ministry is to speak about how the New Testament shapes and determines our corporate identity as the people claimed by and gathered around the cross.

Pastors can also routinely note the ways that all of us have been involved in counter-discipleship by virtue of our inhabiting our various cultures. I was born and raised in the United States—a culture oriented by individual rights that can be asserted when desired or needed. In many ways, because of the manifold effects of the present evil age, ours is a culture of selfishness, of self-seeking, of power and *America* prestige-seeking. All the advertisements I've seen my whole life, along with the many images and messages that enter my mind through social media, reinforce this selfish orientation. I was raised and trained to navigate my way through the world only considering what was best for me, following my own interests and pursuing my own desired ends. All of this is true for those who inhabit my culture along with me. When I preach, therefore, I can note how the way of Jesus runs counter to the ways of life we find in the wider culture. And I don't do this in order to condemn those outside the church, but to cultivate cruciform discernment on the part of those inside the church. I want to explain how cultural dynamics work on our imaginations so that we are pressed to envision living with ourselves at the center.

When we consider matters like divorce or uses of money, we can speak about how people claimed by the cross think about divorce. This is, after all, how Jesus speaks about divorce in Mark 10:1–12 and it shapes Paul's advice to the Corinthians in 1 Corinthians 7. Disciples who are claimed by the cross think about the many contingencies concerning marriage and divorce from their pursuit of discipleship to Jesus. Such a mode of life does not involve pursuing "my needs" and my own personal desires, but rather considers the needs of others, especially those in socially vulnerable situations, such as women.

Rather than touching on every possible topic in Scripture and relating each to cruciformity, I will just note that when I speak about such things in a church setting, I always speak about how we as disciples claimed by the cross conceive of these realities in our world. Our discipleship in the cultures in which we find ourselves trains us to think about all of these matters from the identities we have inherited and our culture's "common sense" ways of thinking. "My money" is mine and I can do with it as I please, right? Well, people claimed by the cross do not think that way. We talk about our money as a gift from God, so we give thanks for it and we seek to use it in a way that flows from and furthers our cruciform discipleship. And when we consider marriage and divorce, we don't consider first "what I need" from this marriage and what I am or am not getting out of it. Rather, we consider how we as people claimed by the cross think about how to treat others. This will radically reshape how we speak about sexual fulfillment—whether and to what extent I am getting my needs met, or whether I am happy with this arrangement. This will lead to different ways of thinking and will reconfigure the questions I ask. All of this will be determined by the cross and how it has claimed my life and is flooding it with resurrection power as God by the Spirit carries me to the day of resurrection.

Preaching, therefore, is one of the main ways that pastors can take the initiative. They can shape a church's imagination so that it is cruciform by preaching about a vast range of topics from this central biblical perspective. This applies most crucially to the "hot button" issues that our culture forces us to confront. The fact that we have not addressed issues such as abortion, human sexuality, parenting, and political involvement from this perspective merely shows that our understanding of the cross has not been faithfully cultivated.

Cruciformity and Church Discipline

A cruciform ministry also takes the initiative when it comes to church discipline. This is probably the area in which most questions regarding cruciformity are raised, in my experience. I have had pastors point out to me that Paul certainly does not seem passive when it comes to church discipline. They assume that cruciformity means that we ought to let people do what they please and not interfere. If Paul calls the Corinthians to put a man out of the church for flagrant sexual sin, shouldn't we take the initiative when it comes to such things?

A cruciform approach to ministry is very helpful here. Rather than conceiving of ministry as passive, pastors are called to remind the church of its identity shaped by the cross and to orient the corporate imagination by the cross. That involves insisting on community dynamics oriented by the cross in the church. The church should be committed to learning how to inhabit community life through intentionally and creatively cultivated behaviors and relational dynamics that are cruciform. The church is a bounded set, constituted by all those who claim an identity marked by the cross. Pastors call everyone toward these corporate dynamics and to consider how they may participate in them.

When members fall into patterns of sin, characterized by behaviors that are not shaped by the cross, pastors, along with anyone else in the church, take the initiative to call them back to their cruciform identity and to cross-oriented practice. They remind sinning members of the hope of experiencing the blessing of participating in the resurrection life and power of God and of moving toward resurrection at the day of Christ. If people insist over time on not living into their cruciform identity, pastors must interpret this in the same cosmic terms we spoke of in chapter 4. Such people are stirring up the dynamics of the present evil age and are acting as agents of the powers of Sin and Death that work destruction in the church. Calls to repent may become more urgent and pastors must have the courage to warn sinning members that the church must be defined by its cruciform identity and that only those who go the way of the cross in obedience to Jesus Christ are welcome in the community.

Grievously, if there are still stubborn refusal to walk in the ways of life and an embrace of destructive practices that lead to death, pastors must have the courage to speak to the rest of the community about this and do so in Pauline terms. Such people see more promise in cultivating habits and patterns that lead to death than in inhabiting cruciform ways of life that lead to resurrection. Of course, the invitation to participate in the enjoyment of resurrection power in the community of God's people is always open to those who return and embrace their cruciform identity. This is done by the cruciform activity of humbly confessing their sin and returning to the cross-shaped behaviors that the church has cultivated. Repentance is a central cruciform practice! And the church embodies its cruciform identity by embracing those who repent and return, freely forgiving them and seeing to it that they do not bear undue burdens of shame.

None of this is passive. This entire approach is cross-determined in that it involves taking the initiative to see to it that the community remains cross-oriented and that anyone in the community who does not see promise and hope in having their life shaped by the cross is put out of the church.

Cruciformity and the "Big" Sins

A third way that pastors can cultivate cruciform modes of ministry is to focus on how Paul conceives of sinful (i.e., not cruciform) patterns of life. In many ways, and for a variety of reasons, in contemporary church contexts "church discipline" usually involves putting people out of the church, or shaming them in some other way, for sexual sin. That is, we tend to operate with a gradation of sins, with adultery, divorce, premarital sex, and use of pornography at the top of the list, and far lesser sins such as gossip and slander hardly meriting a thought that such things would lead to disciplinary action by churches.

It is interesting and instructive to consult Paul's description of the "works of the flesh" in Galatians 5:19–21:

> Now the works of the flesh are obvious: fornication, impurity,
> licentiousness, idolatry, sorcery, enmities, strife, jealousy, anger,
> quarrels, dissensions, factions, envy, drunkenness, carousing, and
> things like these. I am warning you, as I warned you before: those
> who do such things will not inherit the kingdom of God.

Paul does indeed speak of sexual sins, but also lists community conflicts, jealousy, anger, factionalism, and other behaviors that foster
division in the church, alongside apparently heinous sins like sorcery
and drunken carousing. These are all behaviors and patterns of life
that destroy community life and degrade us as humans. Apparently
harmless sinful behaviors like jealousy and anger are behaviors and
attitudes that will keep people from inheriting the kingdom of God.
That is serious!

I have heard countless stories about people who have had to stand
before their churches and confess to sinning sexually or using pornography, and I know of more than a few women who have been
shamed by their churches in the same way for becoming pregnant
out of wedlock. But I cannot recall a single instance of church discipline for being jealous or for persistent and divisive anger. In fact, in
my experience in conservative evangelical churches, I have known
of many people consumed by anger that was manifested in speaking
derisively about others, denouncing them and judging them as less
orthodox and unfaithful to Scripture.

The history of Protestant churches in America, and in many other
places in the Western world, is filled with theological disputes over
doctrine. I can recall church conflicts over the precise formulation
of terms that do not appear in Scripture, such as recent battles over
whether "imputation" is a faithful way to speak of justification by
faith. This calls to mind Paul's exhortation to Timothy in his letter:

> Whoever teaches otherwise and does not agree with the sound
> words of our Lord Jesus Christ and the teaching that is in ac-
> cordance with godliness, is conceited, understanding nothing,
> and has a morbid craving for controversy and for disputes about

words. From these come envy, dissension, slander, base suspicions, and wrangling among those who are depraved in mind and bereft of the truth, imagining that godliness is a means of gain. (1 Tim. 6:3–5)

Paul writes here about people who have a "morbid craving for controversy and for disputes about words," from which flow all sorts of conflicts and divisions. He calls such people "depraved in mind and bereft of the truth." Now, faithfulness to Scripture is indeed important, but many people tend to confuse loyalty to a certain Christian tradition with biblical fidelity. But some of our doctrinal formulations demand greater specificity than can be found in Scripture. Further, commitment to Scripture is determined by ordering our lives by what it says rather than being willing to fight with other people over denominational differences.

The larger point is that Paul called for the church to be cruciform, which calls us all to hold our denominational formulations of doctrine lightly and to embrace and preserve the unity of God's people. Anything that threatens the unity of God's people is something that church leaders ought to regard with utmost seriousness. For Paul, the "big" sins consist of behaviors, attitudes, and patterns of community conduct that threaten unity. Therefore, while not minimizing sexual sins, pastors ought to be on the lookout for any developing dynamics that will ruin community life.

In my opinion, it is worth considering the historical forces that have shaped our imaginations so that we envision sexual sins as the "biggies" and others as far less serious. There is something about historic conservative Christianity in America that is obsessed with sex. I can recall weekend retreats, special meetings at Christian summer camp, and countless sermons in youth group focused on sex and the importance of waiting until marriage. This created church cultures that elevated this area of human experience to such a degree that it has become an obsession. But I can hardly recall sermons on the absolute importance of unity, strategies for avoiding gossip, or the importance of becoming communities that welcome outsiders and serve the poor. Yet, these are the burden of nearly every letter that Paul wrote.

In fact, when Paul, the apostle to the gentiles, met with the leaders of the Jewish Christian church in Jerusalem, it was a tense encounter between leaders who saw things very differently. Paul summarizes that meeting with a note about what all of them regarded as most important:

> On the contrary, when they saw that I had been entrusted with the gospel for the uncircumcised, just as Peter had been entrusted with the gospel for the circumcised (for he who worked through Peter making him an apostle to the circumcised also worked through me in sending me to the Gentiles), and when James and Cephas and John, who were acknowledged pillars, recognized the grace that had been given to me, they gave to Barnabas and me the right hand of fellowship, agreeing that we should go to the Gentiles and they to the circumcised. *They asked only one thing, that we remember the poor, which was actually what I was eager to do.* (Gal. 2:7–10)

When it comes to speaking of sin, therefore, and envisioning behaviors and attitudes that may be subject to church discipline, pastors must consider how Paul thought about sin in light of God's aim to create and sustain unified communities that gather in the name of Jesus. Paul's lists of sins should at least keep us from constructing gradations of sin whereby we pride ourselves on remaining pure sexually while cultivating practices of gossip and slander.

Cruciformity and Knowing Your Limits

Another question that I have come across when I speak about cruciformity comes from worn-out pastors who hear such talk as indicating that they should continue to wear themselves out in ministry. I must say that I hardly meet pastors who are not, to some extent, burned out and frustrated. Is it the case that cruciformity demands ministers exhaust themselves on behalf of the church? Should this sort of talk come as a discouragement? Not at all.

We can make several points about cruciformity that will help us to see that this is the most hopeful reality possible for pastors and ministry leaders. First, being a person claimed by the cross means that God is pouring out resurrection life on me to renew the image of God in me (Rom. 8:29; 2 Cor. 3:18; Eph. 4:24). That involves God's transforming me into a true and renewed human in the image of the Son of God—a human who is enjoying life in God's good world according to his original design. An essential part of that design is following the Sabbath rhythms of creation—work and breaking from work in order to be refreshed. Pastors who are shepherding communities in the way of Jesus, therefore, keep themselves refreshed by following the rhythms of renewed humanity. Sundays are "workdays" for pastors, as they lead communities in celebration of our identity in Christ. They would do well to select some other day on which to take a break from responsible care for the life of the church.

Cruciformity also provides a wonderful framework for considering this. The sources of burnout for many ministers are our ministry ambitions and our fears. On one hand, we may want to see our churches grow, so we forego rest and refreshment and involve ourselves in far more than we should. We push ourselves to do more than we ought to in an effort to cultivate interest in ministries or perhaps to curry favor with someone we hope will remain committed to the church. Alternatively, we may fear that if we're not doing enough, the church will fail. If I don't make this meeting or attend that event, people will notice and I will be subject to criticism. I may want to avoid making someone angry if I maintain my need of refreshment, so I will allow myself to be dragged into more activities than I should.

As someone claimed by the cross, however, I must regard my ambitions, along with my fears, as nailed to the cross, along with any other motivations that keep me from living a truly renewed and refreshing life in Christ. Paul states this theological reality and applies it to another issue, but the truth is just as relevant to the life of pastors:

> Or do you not know that your body is a temple of the Holy Spirit
> within you, which you have from God, and that you are not your
> own? For you were bought with a price; therefore glorify God in
> your body. (1 Cor. 6:19–20)

We are claimed by the cross and we do not have the right to determine our ministry agendas. It takes a clear vision of this reality and the courage provided by the Holy Spirit to maintain our place on the cross, which is the only site on which God pours out resurrection life. Glorifying God in our bodies involves living in such a way that we are enjoying God's sustaining power that is renewing us in the image of Jesus Christ.

Preaching and teaching on the centrality of the cross will also provide a framework to help congregations see the rhythms that pastors have set in their lives. Cruciform pastors are dependent on cruciform churches to give themselves fully to the life of the community so that they can relieve pastors of having to do everything. And if there are community aims and desires that go unfulfilled, that will have to be a reality that pastors and churches accept. Just as an individual pastor's ambitions and fears are nailed to the cross, so, too, are the ambitions, fears and demands of a community. Some programs or dreams may go unfulfilled, but as long as people are taking care to cultivate renewed human patterns of life in order to be re-created in the image of God's Son, then so be it.

Cruciform ministers will learn to know their limits and study their own lives in order to keep themselves in places of refreshment. This will keep us in places of humility. We are not the builders of the church; that task is God's and God's alone. We are agents of his grace and love in the life of the church, but the responsibility for holding on to God's people is his. The church has one Savior, and it is not us! Maintaining this place of humility flows directly from a cruciform identity. Cruciformity, therefore, does not at all mean that we allow ourselves to be pushed and pulled in all directions. It keeps us in the safest possible place—inhabiting the death of Christ so that we may enjoy the life of Christ.

Cruciformity When No One Else Is Interested

Perhaps the most difficult cruciform reality occurs when pastors seek to faithfully occupy their place on the cross when few other people in the church are interested in occupying theirs. Unfortunately, people in our churches may want to make a power move and undermine our ministry in some way. Perhaps a gossip campaign is well underway, or there is a faction on a leadership team that is attempting to corner the pastor in an effort to remove them. Or, there may be a conflict and a fellow leader is manipulating or using strength to get their way. What can be done in such situations?

First, remember to remain cruciform. The temptation will be great to get down from the cross and retaliate against another party that is causing you harm or seeking to injure you in some way. Have the confidence that the cross is the absolute safest place to be. Again, it is the only site upon which God pours out resurrection power. If you step away from the cross, you shut off the supply of God's sustaining power for you, the church, and anyone else involved in a conflict. You are guaranteeing that God's power will not be available for reconciliation and healing.

Resist, then, any and every temptation to answer in kind. As we noted when we discussed Paul's cosmic vision for the life of the church in chapter 4, making any move like that is inviting into the church the corrupting powers of the present evil age and allowing Sin and Death to launch their community-destroying dynamics into the church. You simply cannot entertain taking that course. Remind yourself that doing so would be to put yourself and the church on a course toward destruction, and that course is lined with "deceitful desires" (Eph. 4:22). Such deceptions offer the promise that retaliating or using human strength will sort other people out and put them back in their place. It feels so hopeful to take matters into your own hands and act with strength. But all those tempting feelings and senses are lying to you. Do not listen to them.

Remember that being on a cross will at times—maybe even often—*feel like a cross*. It never was an easy place to be, but rather brought crucified people toward death. You may feel the splinters on your bare back as they dig into your skin, and along with the pain, you may feel alienation and loneliness. That is precisely what it feels like to hang on a cross. Remind yourself that these feelings are not indicators that something is dramatically wrong, but rather that things are going as they should. Remember that on the cross Jesus cried out and demanded to know why God had abandoned him (Mark 15:34). You may feel the same way, even though you are sure you are acting in the right.

Second, prayerfully imagine a range of ways to act from the cross, which is the power of God. Rather than retaliating sinfully, take the initiative to activate cruciform realities, and remember that these will always involve postures of truth-speaking, invitation, and weakness. You can speak the truth that conflict is an opportunity for mutual understanding, but also for possible destruction in the church if not handled carefully. You can invite others into conversation, asking them to explain what they see happening and how they imagine making a way forward. All of these dynamics are ways of embodying the weakness and vulnerability of the cross, opening up the possibility of God pouring out resurrection power that renews and redeems.

Cruciformity is not a method or technique for "getting things done." It is the mode of life to which God calls the church and it is the non-negotiable pattern of life for pastors. It certainly isn't easy or "effective" according to a worldly imagination. But, at the risk of being repetitive, it is the only mode of life upon which God pours out resurrection life on pastors, and through which God blesses the church with his sustaining power.

8

Cruciform Ministry Postures

Throughout this book we have pondered how Paul's encounter with the crucified and exalted Lord Jesus thoroughly transformed the apostle's ministry. That confrontation radically reshaped Paul's conception of himself and his mode of relating to churches so that it was now cruciform—shaped and determined by the cross. We have related that transformation to a range of contemporary ministry dynamics, and in this chapter I will consider how this revolution might shape various ministry postures so that pastors can conceive of how they might situate themselves toward their churches. The goal I have in mind is discerning how cruciformity positions pastors toward their churches.

Deference to What God Is Doing in the Church

Evangelical Christians love using the word "impact." There are conferences named "Impact," books about how Christians impact one another and many organizations and churches seek to "impact the world." I often hear of professors who want to impact students and pastors who want to impact their churches, and want their churches to impact their cities. It seems to me that what Christians are thinking when they use this term is that they want to have *influence* on others—pastors want to influence their churches and they want their churches to have an effect on their surrounding towns and cities.

While this is understandable, it is actually a pretty forceful, even violent, understanding of ministry. The term *impact* has to do with forcefully coming into contact with something, which is a pretty violent understanding of how pastors relate to their churches and how churches relate to the world. Even if we think in terms of something having powerful influence so that something else is changed, this is not really a proper understanding of how we should be thinking of ministry. Paul certainly does not conceive of the pastoral task in this way.

Paul does not seek to impact his churches, nor even to influence them. He is not the active agent determining how his ministry will go, nor the effect he will have on the gentile churches for which he is an apostle. In Paul's view, God is the active agent who builds, grows, and shapes the church. Paul is deferential to God's intentions and plans so that he sees himself as being at God's disposal to do with him as God sees fit. It is instructive to consider some passages in which Paul expresses this deferential posture.

The opening of Paul's letter to the Romans contains his longest greeting to any of his churches. He expresses his desire to visit with them and says something very interesting about his prayers for visiting them:

> For God, whom I serve with my spirit by announcing the gospel
> of his Son, is my witness that without ceasing I remember you
> always in my prayers, asking that by God's will I may somehow
> at last succeed in coming to you. (Rom. 1:9–10)

The NRSV translation makes clear that Paul is praying for God to make a way for him to come to them, leaving a potential visit fully in God's hands.

The Greek text is even more explicit regarding Paul's deference to God's will and prerogative. Below is my translation of Paul's prayer report:

> For God is my witness, whom I worship in my spirit in the gospel
> of his Son, how unceasingly I make mention of you, always in my
> prayers asking whether now at last I will be put on a good path by
> the will of God to come to you. (Rom. 1:9–10)

The Greek verb *euodoō* ("to succeed, to put on a good path") is passive so that Paul is not praying that he might succeed in coming to them. He is not acting here, but *being acted upon*. He is hoping that something will be done *to him*: he prays that he will be put on a good path by God to visit the Roman Christians. The verb can mean something abstract like "to have success," but it is difficult to render that verb as a passive. Robert Jewett opts for a concrete translation, rather than an abstract one, that captures the precise meaning of the verb. Concretely, its meaning is "make a good path,"[1] and in the passive voice means, "to be put on a good path." The point here is that Paul puts himself completely in God's hands, deferring to God alone to determine what Paul will do and when.

We find the same posture in Paul's fascinating little letter to Philemon. Paul's aim in this letter is to reconfigure Philemon's imagination so that Philemon will see his relationship to Onesimus in a completely new way. When he writes about the fracture in Philemon's relationship with Onesimus, he does not mention what Onesimus did—whether he fled from Philemon or refused to return. Rather, he sets the relationship in terms of what God has done by writing in the passive voice:

> Perhaps this is the reason he was separated from you for a while, so that you might have him back forever, no longer as a slave but more than a slave, a beloved brother—especially to me but how much more to you, both in the flesh and in the Lord. (Philem. 15–16)

For Paul, Philemon and Onesimus *were separated*. This is a divine passive, and Paul is inviting Philemon to see God at work. It is God who separated the two for a season, and only did that in order to give Philemon the immense gift of a new brother in the Lord.

At the end of the letter, Paul speaks of his hope to see Philemon at some point in the future. "At the same time also, prepare for me a guest room; for I hope that through your prayers I will be given as a

---

1. Robert Jewett, *Romans*, Hemeneia (Philadelphia: Fortress, 2007), 122.

gift to you" (v. 22, my translation). The verb *charizomai* is again in the passive voice, indicating that Paul is leaving to God the determination of whether or not to give Paul as a gift to Philemon.

Closely related to this, when Paul writes to the Colossians, he does not write about his excitement about the impact that his gospel ministry is having throughout the world. Rather, in a striking passage, he sees the gospel itself as unleashed on the world and doing its powerful work:

> You have heard of this hope before in the word of the truth, the gospel that has come to you. Just as it is bearing fruit and growing in the whole world, so it has been bearing fruit among yourselves from the day you heard it and truly comprehended the grace of God. (Col. 1:5–6)

These passages indicate that Paul envisions God as the active agent of gospel work in the world. God is the one who is building his church, drawing people into the kingdom of God and growing communities into the corporate shape of Jesus Christ by the Spirit. And Paul is deferential to God's will and work.

Paul's conception of how he sees God at work in the world should reorient our imaginations and shape our rhetoric. While I understand what we mean when we say that we want to impact others and have influence, I think that such language betrays a posture in ministry that is unhelpful and may even be destructive.

When we imagine that we want to have impact, either on our churches or surrounding communities, we are posturing ourselves arrogantly. That is, we are arrogating to ourselves places that are not ours to occupy. When we use that language, we imagine ourselves as the people who know what we're doing, who are doing it right and have it all figured out. It is our job to shape other people in our image. If I use that language as a pastor, I am the one who is being a model disciple and it is up to me to forcefully (remember the meaning of "impact") determine the character of the people in my church. And if we use that language as a church, we imagine that we as a church community are the ones who have Christian discipleship figured out and it is our commission to forcefully determine how our surrounding culture ought to live.

In my opinion, people outside the church have gotten the message. While so many churches are doing good work in the world, the arrogant posture of some Christians and churches toward outsiders has made them feel like we are wagging our fingers at them and scolding them for not being like us. Many people feel that Christians have acted hypocritically, that we are always telling others how to behave while we have not always been shining examples of Christian discipleship.

What would it look like to adopt Paul's posture of deference to what God is doing in the church? How might this reconfigure our postures as pastors and the sort of relational dynamics we want to see God cultivate in our communities? One way to reorient our imaginations is to see ourselves as the object of the gospel's work. Rather than imagining that it is our task to change the world, we can imagine that Jesus Christ's task is to change the church through the transforming work of the Holy Spirit. Paul says very little about the church's effect on the wider culture, but he does say that the Lord is working to renew the church:

> And all of us, with unveiled faces, seeing the glory of the Lord as though reflected in a mirror, are being transformed into the same image from one degree of glory to another; for this comes from the Lord, the Spirit. (2 Cor. 3:18)

I see myself as the target of Scripture, the object God is working to transform. I am not armed with the Bible to change others, nor is it my prerogative to shape and determine what is going on in my church. When I change my perspective, I welcome others into my life as the means whereby God is shaping *me*, always transforming *me*.

We can also cultivate our church's corporate imagination so that we see ourselves as the object God is shaping into a gospel community. This is an alternative to seeing ourselves as armed with the gospel to go out and "impact" the world with it. After all, God is building his church and it is not our task to do that for him. But this does not come at the expense of acting in the world. Rather, it reconfigures how we engage with people outside the church. We no longer see them as the objects upon whom the gospel is doing a work. God is working on us, and he just might use our encounters with outsiders to do his work on us. This will reconfigure our posture toward outsiders into one that is far more generous and gracious. It will also keep us from being perceived as hypocrites, since we can speak about our weaknesses and blind spots frankly. We can even ask outsiders to help us identify them so we can open up space for God to transform us even more effectively by the Spirit.

I realize this is utterly counterintuitive to how many people imagine the role of the church in the world. Someone may object, "Well, how else is God going to do his work in the world if it is not through us?" Paul has very little to say about how the church relates to outsiders, and this consists mainly of doing good and cultivating peaceful relationships with them (Rom. 13:1–7; Gal. 6:10; Col. 4:5). It seems to me that we ought to focus on what Paul instructs churches to do rather than what he does not. All of his instruction focuses on cultivating communities that embody and inhabit the reality of the kingdom of God. Nowhere does he indicate that the church should influence or shape the life of the surrounding culture.

Paul is not forceful with his churches and does not portray pastoral ministry as something forceful—certainly not a set of tasks that have "impact." Rather, his posture of humility and service toward his churches unleashes the power of God to transform them. In the same way, churches that embody the counterintuitive kingdom of God will clear space for God to build the church and effect the transformation of the world. We ought to leave to God what only he can do and focus on attending to the instructions Paul gives to the church.

This change of perspective can bear loads of good fruit for pastoral ministry, and for how Christians relate to one another and to outsiders. Just as Paul was open to God giving him as a gift to Philemon, we can learn to see ourselves and others as gifts and open ourselves to the possibility that God may want to give us as gifts to one another.

This way of seeing our participation in the church is so hopeful and confers great dignity on others. When our church gathers, I remain in an open posture toward others without an agenda. I can ask how someone's week has gone and ask good questions that open them up, allowing me to rejoice with their good news or to grieve with their trouble. Alternatively, I can unfold for another person how my week has gone and let them in on my life and my experiences.

Other people have so much to give us and so much capacity to bless us. When Paul imagines the church as a body—the body of Christ—he notes that the sustaining life of God comes to us through other body parts. If I am an elbow, I need the power of God to flow to me through the shoulder, and it passes through me to the hand (Col. 2:19). Participating in the church in this way maintains my connection to Christ, the head of the body.

"Leadership" vs. Responsible Care

It is natural to think of pastors as leaders and to consider what they do as "pastoral leadership." But I have had some growing reservations about this language and all that it implies as it is used to refer to people who serve the church. I am always testing language that is not organic to the Bible to determine whether it contains some hidden assumptions or perhaps orients our imaginations in directions that do not match how Scripture speaks of pastoral ministry. "Leadership" language implies that someone is the leader and they are leading the rest of us somewhere. And what are the rest of us doing? We are *following* the leader.

Now, there are indeed some ways in which this makes good sense of what we find in Paul's letters. Paul does provide a kind of leadership in that he is directing his churches to order themselves in ways that draw upon God's power, and certainly shepherding the church involves leading the flock into relational dynamics that invite God's blessing. Just as shepherds lead their flocks to find nourishing food, pastors also seek to feed their churches on the nourishment provided in Scripture. Leadership, then, does indeed reflect some of the aspects of how Paul conceives of ministry. I have used the language of "ministry leaders" throughout this book because it will connect with those who read it.

It seems to me, however, that leadership language can also be unhelpful when it comes to conceiving of ministry. Primarily, the church follows its ultimate leader, Jesus Christ, who is the Lord and ruler of the church. He is its "head," or the representative who gives to the church its identity and directs the movements of the body. For Paul, faithful church leaders cultivate their communities so they are followers of their only true Shepherd.

Further, I worry that contemporary leadership language fosters a distinction, or separation, between pastors who lead and the ordinary people in the church, giving leaders a sort of exalted status or position of superiority. Perhaps my biggest concern is that so much of the contemporary pastoral leadership literature draws upon leadership principles and practices as these are found in other fields outside of the church, such as business, politics, and education. When we conceive of leadership apart from the specific context of the church we can unconsciously adopt many of the ideologies and assumptions that go along with leadership in these other contexts. We imagine that leaders are bold and decisive entrepreneurial types. We imagine that "successful" leaders build big businesses and lead government agencies, so when we turn to the church, we expect them to be decisive executives, effective administrators, visionaries who know how to make a church grow numerically, magnetically drawing people to follow them with the capacity to motivate.

There is a dramatic difference, however, between pastoral ministry in the church and executive leadership in business. I have paged through Christian leadership books over the years and have often found them filled with advice drawn from leadership principles that work in other fields, using examples from episodes in the Gospels and Paul's life to illustrate them. I can recall reading one book that highlighted Jesus's ability to build a team, citing his work with the twelve disciples as an illustration of how to assemble a leadership team of people who know how to work together. I shook my head in disbelief. Jesus's "team" was probably the worst possible example of the sort of team anyone would put together. Included in the group were Simon the Zealot and Levi the tax collector. Simon would have been committed to the purity of Israel, and Levi would have been regarded as a traitor to his people for collecting taxes for their Roman occupiers (Mark 3:13–19). If anything, the twelve are an instance of Jesus's scandalous behavior and the counterintuitive working of God, who builds his church out of the most unlikely group.

Leadership in the church is utterly unlike that which is found in other social contexts. While pastoral ministry may involve leading to some extent, the main images Paul uses for understanding ministry in the church situate pastors as servants. Paul's apostleship is also dramatically different than the sort of leadership we admire in our wider culture. He does not associate his apostleship with the prestige of leaders in the Roman world, but selects metaphors and images that are humble and even shocking.

In the opening chapters of 1 Corinthians, Paul confronts the church for breaking up into factions that identify with different well-known figures, such as Apollos, Peter and himself. In order to transform their understanding, Paul speaks of his identity and that of his ministry associates:

> What then is Apollos? What is Paul? Servants through whom you came to believe, as the Lord assigned to each. I planted, Apollos watered, but God gave the growth. So neither the one who plants nor the one who waters is anything, but only God who gives the growth. The one who plants and the one who waters have a common purpose, and each will receive wages according to the labor of each. For we are God's servants, working together; you are God's field, God's building. (1 Cor. 3:5–9)

Here, Paul speaks of himself and his partners as servants and field workers. The Corinthians came to believe as God called them and God's servants were merely the means through whom God did this.

Like field workers, they performed various tasks, such as planting and watering, but God is the one who caused organic growth and is the one who continues to sustain them.

Paul notes that they are merely servants of God, workers in God's field. The Corinthians should not identify themselves with Paul, Apollos, or Peter, but with God, for they belong to God alone. They are "God's field, God's building." Paul does not refer to the Corinthians as "mine," or as "my church," "my field," "my building." This is instructive for pastors who have the common practice of speaking about "my church," and "my people." We often speak like this and hear others doing so, too, and we know what we mean. But Paul is careful to remind himself and the Corinthians that they belong to God. Doing so is a reminder to him and to the church that ministers—even apostles—are servants of God's work among them. When they minister, they are doing so on behalf of another and are responsible to God for the work that they do.

Paul then switches to the metaphor of a building, with Paul and the ministers in Corinth as builders.

> According to the grace of God given to me, like a skilled master builder I laid a foundation, and someone else is building on it. Each builder must choose with care how to build on it. For no one can lay any foundation other than the one that has been laid; that foundation is Jesus Christ. Now if anyone builds on the foundation with gold, silver, precious stones, wood, hay, straw—the work of each builder will become visible, for the Day will disclose it, because it will be revealed with fire, and the fire will test what sort of work each has done. If what has been built on the foundation survives, the builder will receive a reward. If the work is burned up, the builder will suffer loss; the builder will be saved, but only as through fire. (1 Cor. 3:10–15)

Paul once again puts himself in the posture of reception—the grace of God was given to him. He is at the disposal of God and has not acted on his own accord. He is the "skilled master builder" who laid the foundation in Corinth of a community shaped by the cross, called into being by God and claimed by the cross of Jesus Christ.

Because the foundation of the church is the word of the cross, each minister that is a builder must carry out their ministry in a way that is consistent with its cruciform foundation. This is crucial because the day of judgment will reveal just what sort of building material each builder has used. The judgment will be rendered by the Lord Jesus Christ, who called the church into being through his death. The cruciform Lord will examine the work of each minister as that building passes through the fires of judgment. The various building materials will be revealed in that fiery evaluation. The gold, silver, and precious stones are ministry modes that are cruciform, and they will survive the scrutiny of the Judge. The wood, hay, and straw will not, for these ministry modes of power and prestige are not consistent with the cross. Such a builder will be saved, says Paul, but the building itself will be burned up.

This vision of ministry is the reason Paul came to the Corinthians in the manner that he did. Rather than shaping his presentation among them to appeal to their desires for impressive rhetoric in order to construct a showy building, he did exactly the opposite.

> When I came to you, brothers and sisters, I did not come proclaiming the mystery of God to you in lofty words or wisdom. For I decided to know nothing among you except Jesus Christ, and him crucified. And I came to you in weakness and in fear and in much trembling. My speech and my proclamation were not with plausible words of wisdom, but with a demonstration of the Spirit and of power, so that your faith might rest not on human wisdom but on the power of God. (1 Cor. 2:1–5)

Paul wanted the Corinthians' faith to rest upon the sure foundation of the cross of Jesus Christ, which is the power of God. Paul's conception of leadership ran directly counter to that of the Corinthian culture. In the same way, contemporary pastoral ministry will not be shaped by how our culture imagines leadership. Such an approach will lead to a devastating judgment at the final day. It is troubling to think of how many of the impressive churches built in our day around powerful personalities will fare when the Lord Jesus Christ renders his searching judgment.

Luke hits these same notes in his portrayal of Paul in Acts 20. On his way to Jerusalem, Paul calls the Ephesian elders to meet with him in Miletus. He charges them solemnly:

> Keep watch over yourselves and over all the flock, of which the Holy Spirit has made you overseers, to shepherd the church of God that he obtained with the blood of his own Son. (Acts 20:28)

We see here again that the church belongs to God—the community "he obtained with the blood of his own Son." Ministers have been appointed by the Holy Spirit as overseers of the flock—shepherds. Just as in 1 Corinthians, Paul here portrays pastoral ministry as "responsible care" for God's people, rather than "leadership." The two images may have quite a bit of overlap at first glance. But the way we imagine "leadership" often contains the notion of an independent figure who is going somewhere and is drawing others to follow along. "Responsible care," however, ties ministers to the church itself, binding them also to God, to whom they will give an account. Ministers and the church belong to God, which gathers them together in a covenantal relationship with God. And that conception of ministry does not allow for a situation in which entrepreneurial types can go their own way and do their own thing.

There are a few other images that Paul uses that further disassociate pastoral ministry from modern conceptions of pastoral leadership. Beverly Gaventa, in her brilliant study of Paul's feminine language regarding his apostleship, notes that Paul chooses some striking images to frame his ministry.[2] He speaks of himself as a woman in labor as he agonizes over the possible departure of the Galatians from the truth of the gospel:

2. Beverly Roberts Gaventa, *Our Mother Saint Paul* (Louisville: Westminster John Knox, 2007).

> My little children, for whom I am again in the pain of childbirth until Christ is formed in you, I wish I were present with you now and could change my tone, for I am perplexed about you. (Gal. 4:19–20)

Further, in 1 Corinthians 3, Paul depicts his ministry in terms of maternal nurture rather than strong masculine authority:

> And so, brothers and sisters, I could not speak to you as spiritual people, but rather as people of the flesh, as infants in Christ. I fed you with milk, not solid food, for you were not ready for solid food. Even now you are still not ready, for you are still of the flesh. (1 Cor. 3:1–3)

This passage, like all of Paul's letters, is loaded with familial imagery, as Paul refers to his audience as "brothers and sisters." But he goes on to depict himself as a nursing mother offering nurturing care for the Corinthians, determining their level of maturity and offering them the appropriate sustenance—milk, rather than solid food.

When he writes to the Thessalonians, Paul contrasts his apostleship with the sort of leadership that the Greco-Roman culture would expect of leaders. He and his partners did not come to the Thessalonians with hidden motives in an attempt to get something from them, nor did they adopt a commanding presence, making demands. He proceeds to associate apostleship with something vastly different:

> As you know and as God is our witness, we never came with words of flattery or with a pretext for greed; nor did we seek praise from mortals, whether from you or from others, though we might have made demands as apostles of Christ. But we were gentle among you, like a nurse tenderly caring for her own children. (1 Thess. 2:5–7).

As Gaventa rightly points out, "Paul draws upon a well-known figure in the ancient world, one identified not only with the nurture of infants but also with continued affection for her charges well into adulthood."[3]

These texts indicate that Paul envisioned pastoral ministry as responsible care. He depicted himself in terms of service, working on God's behalf with communities that belonged to God alone. While we may speak of pastoral ministry in leadership terms, we would do well to be watchful for the worldly ideologies and practices that may be contained in that language. The pastoral task involves nurture and cultivation of communities to take the corporate shape of the cross so they put themselves in position to draw upon the life of God as he pours out resurrection power among them.

Mutuality

Another striking posture we find in Paul's letters is his mutuality—his dependence on ministry associates and his mutual partnership with the churches to which he wrote. We had noted in an earlier chapter that when Paul comments about his former life before his encounter with the exalted Lord Jesus, he saw himself in competition with others. His posture of partnership and dependence on others is a radical change.

In nearly all of his letters, Paul greets his audiences and notes that he is writing along with his fellow workers in mission. In 1 Corinthians, he addresses the church in a letter sent from Paul and Sosthenes (1:1). The second letter is addressed from Paul and Timothy, "our brother" (1:1). He opens his letter to the Colossians in the same way and goes on to speak of how the Colossians heard the truth of the gospel "from Epaphras, our beloved fellow servant" (1:7).

When Paul ministers to churches in the form of letters, he routinely addresses them as part of a ministry team of servants who are also siblings in the family of God along with those to whom he writes. He rhetorically shapes his identity in order to reinforce that while he has a unique role as an apostle, he belongs to others and situates

3. Gaventa, *Our Mother Saint Paul*, 24–25.

himself alongside them rather than over them or apart from them. Because our imaginations are shaped by the examples of strong leadership we see in various other contexts, we envision Paul as a sort of "executive apostle," with others at his disposal, but we do not get this sense *from him*.

We can also see this in how he rhetorically situates himself in a place of dependence on his church audiences. In Romans 1, Paul reports how he is praying that he will be able to come to the Roman Christians at some point in the future, and he anticipates enjoying fellowship with them and being encouraged by them and with them.

> For I am longing to see you so that I may share with you some spiritual gift to strengthen you—or rather so that we may be mutually encouraged by each other's faith, both yours and mine. (Rom. 1:11–12)

In Ephesians, Paul closes the letter by expressing his dependence on the prayers of the churches as he carries out his ministry:

> Pray in the Spirit at all times in every prayer and supplication. To that end keep alert and always persevere in supplication for all the saints. Pray also for me, so that when I speak, a message may be given to me to make known with boldness the mystery of the gospel, for which I am an ambassador in chains. Pray that I may declare it boldly, as I must speak. (Eph. 6:18–20)

This mutuality is highly instructive for contemporary pastors. We noted in an earlier chapter that contemporary ministry in many places is characterized by competitive dynamics. Individual pastors of churches can easily see themselves as competitors with pastors of other churches and can fall prey to the temptation to measure themselves against one another. If someone's church across town is growing, I see that as a threat to me. I am diminished if some other community is flourishing. Pastors in the same town, however, can follow Paul's example by seeing themselves as ministry partners, workers of God in the same field, but perhaps in different corners. We can praise God for the good things we hear happening in another church and offer support and encouragement to fellow ministers. We can form groups of mutual support with pastors of other churches in the same area. Pastors on the staff of a single church can adopt the same posture of mutual support and see to it that a spirit of competition is suppressed.

Pastors can also see themselves as dependent on their churches for their spiritual health, cultivating relationships of mutual dependence. One way to do this is to share preaching opportunities and cultivate the development of ministry teams so that responsible care is shared. Unfortunately, because pastoral ministry is often seen in terms of a career, pastors often adopt postures of self-protection and do not open themselves—and their families—to the spiritual care of the churches they serve.

Paul's pastoral posture toward his churches is instructive in so many ways and on so many levels. He served his churches from a place of weakness and mutuality as he exercised responsible care for them. Pastors who long for their churches to enjoy the presence of Christ, generating among them resurrection power by the Holy Spirit, will creatively emulate Paul rather than the models of leadership we find in our world.

Epilogue

As I mentioned in the preface, I have had the good fortune to engage in conversation with many people in ministry over the material in this book. As I have done so, a number of questions have arisen about the character of cruciformity in ministry, to what extent Paul is an appropriate example for pastors, and how all this relates to service in the contemporary church. In what follows I engage some of these questions.

The Varied Word of the Cross

One question that was raised by a few women in ministry was how the cross speaks a word to them as pastors. I have emphasized how cruciformity calls pastors to embody the narrative trajectory of Christ himself, who did not exploit privileges for personal gain, but rather embarked on a journey of self-expenditure (Phil. 2:5–11). I have articulated how Paul embodied this in his life by not forging his identity according to his privileges and prerogatives, but rather embracing shame and humiliation, positioning himself as a slave, a "sinner," and a servant to his churches.

What I have written raises at least these questions: What about people in ministry who already inhabit social locations of weakness? How does the cross offer hope and promise to women in ministry whose calling is questioned by people in their churches? How does cruciformity affect a person of color who ministers to a mixed-race congregation, serving some who have deep-seated resistance to their efforts? While people who already inhabit marginalized social locations may struggle with misusing power, it is likely that their greater struggle is with the psychological wounds of belittlement. How does a vision of cruciformity speak to them?

These are important questions, about which I offer the following reflections. First, I fully recognize that what I have written in this book is based on my engagement with Paul's vision of cruciformity, how it has reconfigured my inherited vision of ministry, and how it speaks to those who inhabit the social location with which I am familiar. To put it plainly, I have articulated a vision of how the cross speaks to privilege. I am a white man and have never had to justify my place in ministry. All the institutional dynamics of the seminary in which I teach are designed to make me feel comfortable in my place as "professor." I don't have to apologize or explain that I am teaching in a seminary classroom. When I served in pastoral ministry, and even now when I speak in churches, I don't have to answer for myself. It is assumed that what I am doing is "normal." Because of the configuration of pastoral ministry throughout most places in North America, white men occupy pulpits. What I have written in this book will speak most directly to people in those situations.

Second, I am well aware of how rhetoric associated with cruciformity has been sinfully used to keep marginalized people in places of oppression. That is, those in power have kept oppressed people down by drawing on this rhetoric. As just one example, theologians and biblical scholars in America drew upon Scripture in the nineteenth century to maintain the institution of slavery. The same has been done throughout the twentieth century, as white pastors resisted the Civil Rights movement. Currently, a sizeable portion of male pastors and many biblical scholars teach that women should be excluded from pastoral roles. Because of this, I want to recognize that my social location prevents me to a great extent from fully exploring the possibilities of cruciformity for people in ministry who occupy social locations of oppression and marginalization. I have a good idea of how the devastating and renewing word of the cross speaks to me as a white male—and to people like me—but I take my place as a learner and conversation partner to hear how the word of the cross speaks a hopeful and promising word to others. I hope that others

will take up the project of articulating how the cross liberates women
and people of color as they seek to minister to the people of God on
behalf of the God who does not show partiality.

Third, however, there is much to be said for how the word of the
cross offers hope and promise to all those who seek to serve the church
of God. The cross obliterates and re-creates social identities according
to the logic of the kingdom of God. The cross delivers us out of the
present evil age and situates us within the kingdom of God's beloved
Son, a cosmic location in which the first are last and the last are first.
There is a radical reshuffling of social locations so that we now have
our status in the kingdom by virtue of our location in Christ, a place
where there is no longer male or female, slave or free, Jew or gentile, but we all are one in Christ (Gal. 3:28). These social locations no
longer determine our value before God and in this new community.
We are no longer known according to the flesh (2 Cor. 5:16), but are
now known according to the new creation reality of being one new
people (Gal. 6:15). We no longer have our social standing determined
by the standards of the present evil age, which sets us in hierarchies
determined by gender, ethnicity, race, and socioeconomic status.

In Paul's theological vision, this new reality must be embodied
and performed publicly through the church's social ordering. For him,
the reality that Jews and non-Jews in Christ are both welcomed by
God in Christ had to be seen in their enjoying a common meal. If
they did not perform this publicly through a shared meal, then Christ
died pointlessly (Gal. 2:11–21). In the same way, the reality that God
has obliterated and re-created social identities in our day must be
depicted and displayed through the glad celebration of socially marginalized people in places of ministry in the church.

Paul's theological vision of how the cross reorders social realities
in the kingdom of God finds an echo in James's words:

> The brother or sister in a humble social location must celebrate
> their identity in their high status, and the rich must celebrate their
> identity in their humiliated status, because they will pass away
> like a flower of grass. For the sun rises with its heat and with-

ers the grass, and its flower falls and its beauty is destroyed. In the same way the rich will wither away in their pursuits. (James 1:9–11, my translation).

The cross brings the people of God into the new creation and, in doing so, both exalts the lowly and brings low the exalted. While I have articulated a vision in this book of how the cross calls the privileged to inhabit a social station of servitude, those in marginalized social locations can embrace their empowerment as they attend to the hopeful and promising vision of the cross's power to exalt. I believe that those in any social location can benefit from what I have articulated in this book, though the manner in which the cross claims all of us and locates us within God's kingdom may be different. Those at the margins will be resituated at the center. And those in positions of privilege and power will be repositioned alongside their sisters and brothers.

It just may be that churches need to adopt cruciform postures *as communities*, considering how the cross confronts their idolatrous exclusionary practices along gender and racial lines. They can embody resurrection life by becoming places of hospitality, welcoming into pastoral positions gifted people that they might not otherwise have considered.

Did Paul Always Model Cruciformity?

Presenting Paul as a model of cruciformity raises questions about some of his rhetoric. What about his letter to the Galatians in which he twice calls for God to curse those who disagree with him (Gal. 1:8–9)? In this letter, he reports a tough confrontation of Peter in Antioch (2:11–14), and exhorts his opponents in Galatia to castrate themselves (5:12). How cruciform is that? It is difficult to read his letter to Philemon and come away with any other impression than that he was coercing him to accept Onesimus. Was Paul being manipulative? Can we really say that Paul is a model for how we should embody cruciformity in ministry?

Again, these are great questions, and all I can offer is my perspective on them. Regarding his tough rhetoric in Galatians, I think it is important to keep in mind that there is a great difference between Paul and the rest of us. First, he was an apostle who had a clear-eyed conception of the liberating power of the one true gospel. His discernment, therefore, of theological error that would have massive practical consequences, puts him in a different class from the rest of us. He was not merely engaging in doctrinal debate across denominational lines or debating between theological schools of thought based on his letters the way we do. His rhetoric, therefore, may not be an appropriate model for us to follow. Our judgments are often clouded, and we inevitably have theological and traditional commitments that don't always allow us to see clearly the merits of sisters and brothers who think differently than we do.

Second, beyond merely engaging in theological debate, Paul knew that the "other gospel" that was being promulgated among the Galatians would have led to great social upheaval in those churches. The Galatians were being told that they had to adopt an ethnic identity that was entirely foreign to what they knew. All aspects of their lives would dramatically change, and in a way that was different from their entrance into the faith. This would have profoundly destabilized their communities and upset their lives, fracturing the unity that God had created in Christ. Their experience of being Christian would have been anything but liberating. It would have enslaved them. His white-hot rhetoric is driven by his knowledge that they were being led back into captivity, away from freedom (4:9). He is a pastor, and he writes passionately because he longs for their flourishing. He is not interested in scoring points in an abstract theological debate.

Third, I wonder if, when considering Paul's report of his confrontation with Peter in Antioch (2:11–14), we have been affected more by Hollywood depictions of heroism than by what Paul actually writes. He notes that when Peter came to Antioch, "I opposed him to his face, *because he stood self-condemned*" (2:11). Peter's error in refraining from table fellowship with non-Jews sent the message to the Galatians that they stood outside the people of God because of their ethnicity. Again, Paul's pastoral heart is on display in his care for the Galatians and his concern for their enjoyment of God's order of flourishing and blessing. He only confronted Peter because Peter's actions put him in the place of condemnation—he was pulling Peter back from a place of God's judgment! Rather than envisioning a scenario in which Paul jumps up on a table and dramatically grabs Peter's robe and loudly shouts him down, we might imagine that Paul acted courageously and spoke clearly and plainly. He identified how Peter was "not acting consistently with the truth of the gospel" (2:14), and called him and the other Jewish Christians to a better way.

In all of this, Paul put himself on the line so that the Galatians could inhabit the freedom of the gospel. *That is the heart of cruciformity.* Paul was not a hothead who failed to control himself in the midst of theological debate, but rather a pastor who acted with courage and conviction in service to the good of others.

But what about Philemon? Was Paul manipulative or coercive with him? I must say, as a middle-class white person, that Paul's letter seems to resonate with the passive-aggressive communication style that many of us know all too well!

But I think this lovely little letter to Philemon is actually a perfect example of pastoral care and counsel. It all starts with Paul's report of how he prays for Philemon, especially the often poorly translated verse 6:

> I give thanks to my God, always making mention of you in my prayers, hearing of your love and faithfulness which you have toward the Lord Jesus and unto all the saints, and I pray that your sharing in faithfulness will become effective in the knowledge of all the good that God works among us unto Christ. (Philem. 4–6, my translation)

Paul commends Philemon warmly and informs him that he is praying for him, especially that his identification with Christ will result in his acting in this situation *toward Christ*. He is referring specifically to the challenging prospect of what to do with Onesimus, who in some way has brought harm to Philemon.

Paul has sent Onesimus back to Philemon in hopes that he will receive him warmly and forgive him (v. 17). Philemon will be tempted to treat Onesimus harshly in some way, perhaps even punishing him by death. In that way Philemon could publicly identify himself as one loyal to the socio-political order of Rome—acting as if Caesar were the true lord of the cosmos, rather than Christ. His punishing of Onesimus, as his social peers would probably expect, would uphold Roman values and preserve Philemon's social honor. Paul is exhorting him, however, to act in this situation "toward Christ"—behaving as if Christ is Lord despite what it might cost Philemon in the loss of social status and, therefore, economic prospects.

In Paul's view, Philemon faces a situation in which he is tempted to act in such a way that would deny his fidelity to the Lord Jesus Christ, and that is not an option that Paul entertains. Neither will he allow Philemon to consider it. He reframes the conflict between Philemon and Onesimus and invites Philemon to consider it from the perspective of God orchestrating an opportunity to give Philemon the gift of a new brother in the Lord:

> Perhaps this is why he was separated from you for a while, so that you might have him back forever, no longer as a slave but more than a slave, a beloved brother—especially to me but how much more to you, both in the flesh and in the Lord. (Philem. 15–16)

Indeed, Paul goes on to rhetorically configure the situation for Philemon so that he does not have another option other than warmly welcoming Onesimus. In my opinion, however, this is not manipulative. In Paul's view, to behave in any other way than "toward Christ" is not something Philemon can consider. The course he must take is obviously a tough one. But Paul is a pastor counseling a professing Christian who is considering retaliation against a brother in order to preserve his social status.

Again, Paul puts himself on the line with Philemon, offering to repay whatever Onesimus owes to Philemon (v. 19). And yes, Paul does mention that Philemon in some way owes to Paul his "very own self"

(v. 20), but this is an instance of the solidarity that all believers share in Christ. Philemon, Onesimus, and Paul all belong to each other in Christ, so none of them can consider violence against another part of the body.

If we were to imagine a contemporary situation in which someone had come to us for counsel before they took an obviously sinful and self-destructive course of action, we would do well to consider Paul's rhetorical strategy with Philemon. We may likewise offer ourselves in solidarity, putting ourselves on the line to participate with that person in a potentially difficult set of steps that embodied discipleship to Jesus. In such cases, the stakes for a professing Christian are high. Pastors do not let people consider walking in disobedience as a viable option.

Many writers on a variety of topics have shaped my thinking about Paul and pastoral ministry over the last three decades. I commend the following to those looking for further reading.

When I was finishing seminary and writing a thesis on Galatians, Bruce Longenecker's *The Triumph of Abraham's God: The Transformation of Identity in Galatians* (Nashville: Abingdon, 1998) completely reconfigured my understanding of Paul. This book introduced me to the upside-down and paradoxical manner in which God triumphed over hostile cosmic powers in the crucified Christ. This was also my first encounter with the notion of cruciformity, the church's mode of inclusive community life that "advertises God's transforming power and overlordship in Christ" (p. 67). I later studied with Bruce for my PhD at the University of St. Andrews, and my subsequent book, *The Drama of Ephesians: Participating in the Triumph of God* (Downers Grove, IL: IVP Academic, 2010), indicates his influence on my thought. I would also mention Longenecker's fictional work, *The Lost Letters of Pergamum: A Story from the New Testament World*, 2nd ed. (Grand Rapids: Baker Academic, 2016), which introduces readers to the kind of cruciform community life that the gospel creates.

N. T. Wright's *What Saint Paul Really Said: Was Paul of Tarsus the Real Founder of Christianity?* (Grand Rapids: Eerdmans, 1997) was influential in helping me understand Paul's aims before his conversion. His chapter on "Saul the Persecutor, Paul the Convert," shed great light on the sort of zealous "ministry mode" Saul carried out. This book, and his subsequent works on Paul, determine to a great extent how I have portrayed Paul's preconversion mode of ministry, driven by pursuits of power and prestige.

Michael Gorman's work on cruciformity, in at least two books, highlights how Philippians 2:5–11 plays a central role in Paul's theology, and this has left a major imprint on my thinking about Paul and the discussions throughout this book. Particularly important are *Cruciformity: Paul's Narrative Spirituality of the Cross* (Grand Rapids: Eerdmans, 2001) and *Inhabiting the Cruciform God: Kenosis, Justification, and Theosis in Paul's Narrative Soteriology* (Grand Rapids: Eerdmans, 2009).

Marva Dawn's *Powers, Weakness, and the Tabernacling of God* (Grand Rapids: Eerdmans, 2001) is a beautiful reflection on the character of the powers and how they seduce us to pursue power and prestige. She draws upon Paul's discussion of power and weakness in 2 Corinthians 12:9 and relates Paul's embodiment of weakness to a range of practices for the church to experience God's dwelling among us. Her warning to churches to avoid the seductions that draw us into the strategies of the hostile cosmic powers resonated powerfully with me and helped me to see the ways that churches and Christian organizations fall prey to quests for power.

Beverly Roberts Gaventa's *Our Mother Saint Paul* (Louisville: Westminster John Knox, 2007) is a vigorously exegetical and richly theological treatment of Paul's portrayal of his apostleship with reference to his churches. She notes how he adopts social locations of weakness and humiliation to posture himself as a nurturer of his communities. Her work offers rich resources for reconsidering the manner in which so many view Paul's apostleship as an office of "authority." If this is not how Paul views his identity and task with regard to his churches, then we ought to revisit the inherited frames through which we see him doing his work. After all, this conception powerfully affects how we understand the pastoral task.

Like the foregoing scholars, James Thompson is a veteran exegete and student of Paul who has given sustained attention to Paul's letters and how they shape contemporary ministry. Two of his books in particular offer rich material for reflection on the pastoral task: *The Church according to Paul: Rediscovering the Community Conformed to Christ* (Grand Rapids: Baker Academic, 2014) and *Pastoral Ministry according to Paul: A Biblical Vision* (Grand Rapids: Baker Academic, 2006).

Scot McKnight is another seasoned exegete and senior New Testament scholar who has turned to writing for the church over the last few decades. His recent work, *Pastor Paul: Nurturing a Culture of Christoformity in the Church* (Grand Rapids: Brazos, 2019), focuses on pastors as culture makers. McKnight's work is the result of participating for years in the guild of biblical scholarship while also remaining in touch with the pressing concerns and needs of pastors, to whom and with whom he often speaks. This book is an excellent place to start to gain a broad vision of the pastoral task.

In my opinion, it is critical for pastors to attend to the biblical text while also discerning the dynamics of our current culture. We can observe how Paul speaks to the perverted ideologies and corrupted cultural patterns of his day, but we must also understand those that powerfully affect our mindsets and prevent our communities from flourishing. I have sought to be a critical student of my present cultural moment, seeking to discern the assumptions and mindsets that are up and running in our world and that shape the hopes and fears of Christian culture.

Daniel Boorstin's brilliant *The Image: A Guide to Pseudo-Events in America* (New York: Vintage, 1992) initially hooked me on cultural criticism. I have returned to it many times over the last several decades, and while it was originally published in 1961, it is fundamental to understanding the dynamics of public relations and image maintenance that continue to affect us today. A careful consideration of his analysis would be an ideal place to begin to comprehend the many ways in which social media have determined how we think about ourselves in relation to others. Many of my reflections on pastoral ministry in an age dominated by social media have their genesis in Boorstin's observations.

Alain de Botton's *Status Anxiety* (New York: Vintage, 2005) examines the pervasive culture of comparison with others and the subtle sense of unease that infects us when we feel that others are bypassing us on the quest for upward mobility. Competitive pursuits powerfully affect pastors who judge themselves by one another in terms of accomplishment and congregational size. While this book is not written from a Christian perspective, it sheds light on how comparison with others robs us of joy and distracts us from the pastoral task.

Several other classics of popular social analysis have informed my thinking about pastoral ministry in this era, including Barry Glassner,

The Culture of Fear: Why Americans Are Afraid of the Wrong Things, rev. ed. (New York: Basic Books, 2018); Sherry Turkle, *Alone Together: Why We Expect More from Technology and Less from Each Other*, rev. ed. (New York: Basic Books, 2017); Christopher Lasch, *The Culture of Narcissism: American Life in an Age of Diminishing Expectations* (New York: Norton, 1991).

I am convinced that it is crucial for pastors to understand the history of Christianity in America, especially the character of American evangelicalism, which is so entwined with the American narrative. Many good works are available to tell this story from various perspectives. An important starting point is George Marsden's *Fundamentalism and American Culture*, 2nd ed. (New York: Oxford University Press, 2006). His *Reforming Fundamentalism: Fuller Seminary and the New Evangelicalism* (Grand Rapids: Eerdmans, 1995) is an account of the resurgent evangelical movement that sought cultural approval and academic prestige. Also well worth consulting is Joel Carpenter's *Revive Us Again: The Reawakening of American Fundamentalism* (New York: Oxford University Press, 1997). These works offer a glimpse into the period of incubation in the middle of the twentieth century that formed the present evangelical culture.

Frances FitzGerald provides a broad historical survey of evangelical life from the founding of the republic to the present in her magisterial *The Evangelicals: The Struggle to Shape America* (New York: Simon and Schuster, 2017). She especially highlights the evangelical urge to control the course of American history and traces the origins of the political agitation we now see so clearly. Two more recent works by historians are important for coming to grips with the current shape of evangelical life and culture: Matthew Avery Sutton's *American Apocalypse: A History of Modern Evangelicalism* (Cambridge, MA: Belknap Press, 2014), and Kevin M. Kruse, *One Nation Under God: How Corporate America Invented Christian America* (New York: Basic Books, 2016).

Subject Index

Agassi, André, 87
ambition, 24, 30, 71, 128–29

baptism, 120
Barnabas, 51
believers: identity of, 104, 119–20,
121, 122, 141, 150; marginalized,
149, 150–51
blasphemy, 19–20
boasting, 94–96, 97, 98, 101, 104, 105
burnout, 127–28. *See also* limits,
personal

calling, 111–12, 113–14
capitalism, 32
celebrity: association with, 27, 57,
65, 89, 90, 108; credentials and,
29, 88–91, 108; ministry liabilities
of, 65, 108; Paul's postconversion
view of, 58, 61, 65, 88–91
church/community: ambitions and
desires of, 129; cosmic context of,
7–9, 48–50; cruciform patterns
and practices in, 10, 47–49, 62,
78–79, 120–21, 131; expectation of
hope in, 84–86; as family, 32–33;
identity of, 119–20; needs of,
30–32; relationship to power, 79;
as resurrection presence, 8, 9–10,
46–49, 61, 77–78; size of, 106; social order in, 150–51; unity of, 126

church discipline, 123–24, 125
community. *See* church/
community
competition, spirit of, 24–25, 73–75,
146–47
conflict resolution, 81–84
cosmic enslavement: characteris-
tics of, 73–74; in contemporary
ministry, 8, 65, 74–76, 81; desire
for power and, 69, 73, 74; forces
driving, 71, 72, 76; impact of, 8;
Jesus's victory over, 7–8, 76–77,
79; Paul's preconversion relationship to, 74
cosmic worldview: as context for
church, 7–9, 48–50; ministry
postures and, 66–67, 74–76, 81,
83; new creation, 45–46, 67–68,
76–77, 80; rulers of, 68–72. *See
also* Paul, cosmic view of
credentials: academic degrees as,
23, 106–7, 114, 117, 118; boasting/
self-promotion and, 94–96, 97;
celebrity and, 29, 88–91, 108;
church size as, 106; competitive spirit and, 24–25, 106; in
contemporary ministry, 23, 29, 65,
106–8, 113–15; cosmic significance
of, 65; cruciformity and, 108–15,
118; Jesus's lack of, 36; versus justification by faith, 117–18; of Paul,

161

Scripture Index